FLORIDA GATORS

2006 NCAA CHAMPIONS

The Gainesville Sun

SPORTS
PUBLISHING
L.L.C.

SportsPublishingLLC.com

Publishers
Peter L. Bannon and Joseph J. Bannon Sr.

Senior Managing Editor
Susan M. Moyer
Coordinating Editor
Joseph J. Bannon Jr.
Developmental Editor
Erin Linden-Levy

Art Director
K. Jeffrey Higgerson
Book and Cover Design
Dustin Hubbart
Book Layout and Imaging
Heidi Norsen

The Gainesville Sun

Publisher
James E. Doughton

Executive Editor
James R. Osteen

Managing Editor
Jacalyn Levine

Contents

Welcome Note

Dear Reader:

This was a magical season that no one saw coming. A young, unproven, but talented Gator basketball team started the season with a record string of victories, suffered a bit of a swoon, then rallied to win a second straight Southeastern Conference tournament championship. What happened next will live forever in the annals of Gator Nation lore. The first ever NCAA title capped the most remarkable year in Gator men's basketball history. Coach Billy Donovan and his team have brought the Gator Nation a most memorable season and are to be congratulated for this wonderful achievement.

The Gainesville Sun and gatorsports.com have covered every step of this historic journey from the preseason games to the early wins in New York's Madison Square Garden to the final buzzer in Indianapolis. We're pleased to offer Gators fans this book, which celebrates this season to remember.

Through these pages, we hope you will relive the special moments and games and be reminded of all the twists and turns which made this season such a miraculous one. This book draws upon the outstanding articles, columns and photographs of our talented staff and illustrates the commitment of *The Sun* to provide the best possible coverage of Gator sports.

We hope you will enjoy every page.

Jim Doughton
Publisher, *The Gainesville Sun*

Jim Osteen
Executive Editor, *The Gainesville Sun*

Michael C. Weimar/The Gainesville Sun

DONOVAN'S CREATION

By KEVIN BROCKWAY

They were the unquestioned big three of the Florida basketball program.

For two years, the faces of Florida basketball were clutch-shooting point guard Anthony Roberson, curly haired shooting guard Matt Walsh and rebound-machine forward David Lee. Florida coach Billy Donovan served as the fourth face on the Rushmore of the Gator basketball landscape, bringing along the three scorers and egos through their respective growing pains.

The era ended with the first Southeastern Conference Tournament title in school history, but no closer to a national title than when Florida made its historic run to the NCAA Finals under Donovan in 2000. For the fifth straight year, Florida was knocked out of the NCAA Tournament in the first weekend. The second-round loss to Villanova was a crushing blow, one that reduced Walsh to tears and left Lee and Roberson in dazed silence as they left the court.

All three knew the window had closed. Lee, a senior, graduated. Walsh and Roberson, both juniors, left as underclassmen.

Donovan is left this season with a new team he can mold, a group that may need to rely on each other more than in past seasons. Last year's freshman class, led by returning starters Corey Brewer and Al Horford, will be expected to grow up quickly. More will be asked of sophomores Taurean Green and Joakim Noah, and returning juniors Chris Richard and Lee Humphrey.

"As time goes on you're always going to lose guys," Donovan said. "When I first got to Florida it was Eddie Shannon, Greg Stolt and Kenyan Weeks, then it was Mike Miller, and (Udonis) Haslem and those guys and then obviously it was David Lee and Walsh and Roberson.

"Now, we've got a core of guys. It's that next stage, and guys are moving into different roles than they did a year ago. I think last year they came in,

ABOVE: Chris Richard demonstrates his dunking skills over a volunteer from the women's basketball team.

Briana Brough/The Gainesville Sun

PRESEASON

ABOVE: During Midnight Madness, Corey Brewer dazzles the crowd with his vertical leap. *Briana Brough/The Gainesville Sun*

they filled a void, they brought competitiveness and toughness and defense and rebounding to make our team better. But now they are going to have to take over a bigger and maybe a little bit more of a major role."

With Roberson, Walsh and Lee, there was little doubt as to where the points were going to come from. The three accounted for close to 60 percent of

Florida's scoring last season. The plays ran through them. In crunch time, one of the three was going to get the ball.

The challenge, Donovan acknowledged, will be diffusing the pressure that comes with losing three proven scorers.

"If we can have four to five guys get between 10 to 14 points a game, then that scoring loss that we suffered this past year will offset itself," Donovan said. "The question I keep hearing from everybody is who is emerging, who is the guy. There is no guy. There really isn't. I think it's got to be our team."

That means Brewer may have to score 19 points one night, Horford 17 the next and Humphrey maybe 18 in a game the following week. It likely won't produce the same numbers that had Florida near the top of most offensive categories in the Southeastern Conference during the Walsh-Roberson-Lee era. Florida may have to rely on out-slugging teams this season more than outscoring them.

"Are we going to have some games where we're going to go through some droughts? Yeah. But I'm really not worried about the scoring, per se," Donovan said. "I really can't control that. I think the big thing for me is as long as we're getting good shots."

Donovan will have to strike a balance in giving his new scorers some freedom. With it comes responsibility.

"The biggest thing is getting them to the point where they understand the shots they can make," Donovan said. "The last thing I want is for those guys to be tentative or tight offensively. I want them to play with freedom, I want them to play loose and I want them to have fun."

Defensively, Florida is athletic enough to get back to a staple of the Donovan era when he first took over the program nine years ago. Florida should be able to press more this year. Speeding up the tempo with the press might also get the offense on track through some early struggles.

With Walsh, Roberson and Lee, it was about conserving energy for the latter part of games. With this group, it will be about creating it.

"I think it's going to be a lot more up-and-down basketball, a very fast game. But, we'll see," Noah said. "As long as we get the 'W' it doesn't matter how we get it. As long as we get it."

Brewer, a hard-nosed perimeter defender, envisions a team that will win games with defense as often as it will with offense.

"We're going to be doing down and dirty," Brewer said. "We're going to do all the little things."

There's strength in the frontcourt, particularly if Noah and Richard translate improvement in practice this fall to their play on the court. Florida could develop into a team that gets fouled more often, but the frontcourt players will need to improve their free-throw shooting in order to successfully cash in. Brewer shot 58.1 percent from the line last season. Horford shot 58.2 percent and Noah shot 57.7 percent.

Regardless, players seem excited about the chance to create a different image. Donovan said the team is hustling and listening in practice. Players have embraced their current underdog status.

"I think there are guys on this team excited about the opportunity of taking on some new roles," Humphrey said. "You don't know what to expect, but we feel pretty good about where we are in practice. We feel like we have a chance to do some exciting things."

NOVEMBER 18, 2005

MADISON SQUARE GARDEN, NEW YORK, NEW YORK

BIG APPLE BASH

By **KEVIN BROCKWAY,** *Sun sports writer*

Florida came into the second round of the 2K Sports College Classic Benefiting Coaches vs. Cancer eager to prove a point.

The Gators did it in a big way on one of the biggest stages of college basketball. For the second straight night, Florida beat a ranked team, downing No. 16 Syracuse 75-70 at Madison Square Garden to win the tournament for the first time in school history.

Again, it was Taurean Green coming up with the big shots in the clutch for Florida (4-0). Green matched his career-high scoring output from Wake Forest with 23 points, five coming during a deciding 10-0 run that closed the game.

Green began the run with an assist, feeding Chris Richard on a dunk to put Florida up 64-62 with 5:39 remaining. The Gators never trailed after that. Green hit a pull-up jumper to extend the lead to 66-62.

After Al Horford made one of two free throws, Richard scored again on a lay-in and Green hit a three-pointer with 1:48 left to clinch it at 72-62.

Syracuse (3-1) got a career-high 24 points from Demetris Nichols, but went cold down the stretch. Meanwhile, five Florida players reached double figures.

After a wild first half that saw Florida down 44-43 at halftime, the Gators made a push by going inside to Horford and Joakim Noah during an early, 11-0, second-half run. Horford scored consecutive baskets on a lay-up and dunk to put Florida ahead 49-47. Noah followed with four consecutive three throws and Green's three-pointer from the right side extended Florida's lead to 56-47 with 16:07 remaining.

But the Gators went cold during a five-minute scoreless stretch that had its share of chippy moments. Freshmen Eric Devendorf of Syracuse and Walter Hodge of Florida were whistled for a double technical during a scrum for the loose ball.

OPPOSITE PAGE: Corey Brewer (left) and Taurean Green exchange congratulations in the final seconds of their Coaches vs. Cancer tournament game against Syracuse. Green was named tournament MVP. *AP/WWP*

Devendorf, whose final two school choices were Syracuse and Florida, cut Florida's lead to 56-54 with a runner in the lane. Syracuse tied it on a bank shot by Roberts, but Horford ended the drought with a 14-foot jumper to put Florida back up 58-56.

Playing its first game against Syracuse since 1987, Florida went back-and-forth with the Orangemen during a first half that included seven ties and 10 lead changes.

Florida attacked Syracuse's 2-3 zone early by shooting over it. The Gators went 8-of-17 from the three-point line in the first half, offsetting seven missed free throws.

The sea of partisan Syracuse orange that filtered into the Garden heckled Florida throughout. The emotional Noah was their favorite target, especially after he pumped his fist on his chest in front of some orange shirts that he must have mistook for Florida supporters.

Both teams waited through two overtimes from winner Wake Forest and Texas Tech before the 9:40 opening tip. The late start didn't affect the shooting on either side. Green started the early perimeter barrage with a three from the right side to put Florida up 7-4. Nichols answered with a three-pointer for Syracuse.

Lee Humphrey sank his first three-pointer from NBA range at the 15-minute mark to put Florida up 14-9. Humphrey followed with two more threes with in a two-minute stretch. Again, Syracuse

turned to Nichols, whose three pulled the Orangemen within 20-19. Green ended the flurry with his second three to put Florida back ahead by four.

A Richard dunk gave Florida its largest lead of the half, 41-36, but Syracuse closed the half with an 8-2 run. Roberts began it with a dunk off a pretty feed from McNamara. Louie McCrosky made 1 of 2 free throws and then fed Roberts for another dunk to tie the score at 41. After a Noah turnover, Nichols sank his fourth three-pointer of the half, giving the Orangemen their first lead since the six-minute mark. Brewer made a short turnaround with 5.8 seconds left to pull Florida within 44-43 at halftime.

	1st	2nd	Total
Syracuse	44	26	70
Florida	43	32	75

Syracuse

Player	FGM-A	3FGM-A	FTM-A	O-D REB	TP	A	BLK	S
Roberts	6-16	0-1	0-0	5-2	12	3	1	1
Nichols	8-16	5-10	3-4	1-4	24	2	0	1
Watkins	2-5	0-0	0-0	3-5	4	0	4	1
McNamara	5-19	3-11	0-0	2-1	13	10	0	0
McCroskey	2-7	0-0	1-2	3-6	5	2	0	1
Onauku	0-0	0-0	0-0	0-1	0	0	0	0
Devendorf	3-7	0-3	4-4	1-1	10	0	0	0
Gorman	1-2	0-0	0-0	1-0	2	0	0	0
Wright	0-0	0-0	0-0	0-0	0	0	0	0
Totals	27-72	8-25	8-10	16-20	70	17	5	4
	(37.5%)	(32.0%)	(80.0%)					

Florida

Player	FGM-A	3FGM-A	FTM-A	O-D REB	TP	A	BLK	S
Brewer	2-9	0-3	1-4	2-7	5	4	1	2
Noah	4-6	0-0	4-6	2-5	12	2	2	4
Horford	5-7	0-0	1-4	0-4	11	2	2	0
Green	7-12	6-9	3-5	0-2	23	6	0	1
Humphrey	4-9	4-9	1-4	2-2	13	2	0	0
Moss	0-0	0-0	1-2	1-0	1	0	0	0
Hodge	0-5	0-2	0-0	2-0	0	0	0	1
Richard	4-5	0-0	2-2	3-2	10	0	0	0
Huertas	0-0	0-0	0-0	0-1	0	0	0	0
Totals	26-53	10-23	13-27	12-23	75	16	5	8
	(49.1%)	(43.5%)	(48.1%)					

NOVEMBER 25, 2005

O'CONNELL CENTER, GAINESVILLE, FLORIDA

'NOLE KNOCKDOWN

By KEVIN BROCKWAY, *Sun sports writer*

Florida point guard Taurean Green couldn't recall a game when he shot more free throws. Florida State coach Leonard Hamilton couldn't recall a game when three different players fouled out.

In another wacky turn to the Florida-Florida State men's basketball rivalry, the 14th-ranked Gators survived an upset threat by keeping their composure late in a 74-66 win that had its share of surreal moments.

In front of a sellout crowd at the O'Connell Center, Florida (5-0) battled back from a 21-4 hole to win the in-state rivalry for the seventh time in eight meetings.

"We knew coming in this was going to be a tough, physical game," Green said. "They played us that way last year. We knew we had to play physical back."

Green led Florida with 15 points, all coming at the free-throw line. Al Horford added 14 points, Corey Brewer scored 13, Lee Humphrey scored 12 and freshman Walter Hodge added 10 off the bench as five players reached double figures for Florida for the third time in five games.

"We have a lot of room for improvement," Florida coach Billy Donovan said. "One thing I can say for Florida State is I have lot of respect for the competitors they are."

Humphrey put Florida up to stay 60-58 with a three-pointer with 5:11 remaining. The Gators went on to score the next nine points as Florida State (2-1) faltered late in the half.

OPPOSITE PAGE: Corey Brewer throws down a fast-break dunk over the Seminoles. *Michael C. Weimar/The Gainesville Sun*

throughout. The Seminoles held Florida to a season-low 45 percent from the floor, but couldn't come up with enough points late.

"Once we got in foul trouble, we had odd line-ups on the floor and never seemed to be able to maintain any kind of rhythm," Hamilton said. "We were OK in transition, but once we got into half-court, we didn't execute as we had planned."

Green made 15 of 16 free-throw attempts, tying Andrew Moten (1985) for an O-Dome record for made free throws. Florida, which entered the game shooting 57.4 percent from the line, made 22 of 27 second-half free throws to finish 73.3 percent (33-45) for the game.

Donovan warned earlier in the week that any college basketball team was vulnerable. In front of a frenzied full house, Florida played the first half to his prophecy.

Sparked by eight straight points from Thornton, Florida State jumped to a 10-0 lead before Florida scored its first point on a Brewer free throw at the 15:43 mark. Florida missed its first five shots, turned the ball over twice and had no second-chance points during the brutal game-opening stretch.

"We were impatient in our offense," Donovan said. "I don't know if it was the crowd, the emotion, we just didn't do as good a job at the start of this game as we had in previous games."

Brewer (6 assists) found Horford underneath the basket for a dunk to extend Florida's lead to 64-58. Chris Richard followed with a lay-up and Green, who made all 14 of his second-half free throws, hit two more after he was fouled by FSU guard Todd Galloway driving to the basket.

Senior guard Andrew Wilson led Florida State with 13 points. Galloway added 11 and leading scorer Al Thornton scored nine, eight coming in the first half.

Wilson, Galloway and center Alexander Johnson all fouled out as FSU played physical

ABOVE: With a roar, Corey Brewer celebrates as the Gators swamp the Seminoles. Brewer notched 13 points and six assists on the night. *Michael C. Weimar/The Gainesville Sun*
OPPOSITE PAGE: Al Horford (right) battles for possession with a Florida State player. *Michael C. Weimar/The Gainesville Sun*

lift off the bench, sinking two straight three-pointers to pull Florida within 24-10.

The shots opened things up inside. Florida scored eight straight points on a Joakim Noah dunk, a Horford put-back and four free throws. Wilson ended Florida's 11-0 run with a lay-up that put Florida State up 26-18.

A turn-around jumper by Brewer cut FSU's lead to 30-28, but the Seminoles closed the half out on an 8-2 run, taking a 38-30 to halftime.

"I was disappointed we were down by eight at the half," Donovan said. "In the second half, we executed a lot better."

Wilson threatened to bury the Gators, sinking three straight three-pointers during a three-minute span. The third extended Florida State's lead to 24-7, its largest of the half.

"I wasn't worried," Horford said. "It's a 40-minute game. They got off to a good start and I guess we got too excited and weren't doing the little things."

From there, Florida whittled away. Hodge, who came into the game 1 for his first 15, gave Florida a

	1st	2nd	Total
Florida State	38	28	66
Florida	30	44	74

Florida State

Player	FGM-A	3FGM-A	FTM-A	O-D REB	TP	A	BLK	S
Thornton	4-8	0-1	1-2	0-1	9	0	0	0
Johnson	1-4	0-1	1-4	2-3	3	1	1	0
Swann	2-8	1-6	0-0	0-2	5	3	0	2
Galloway	4-7	1-1	2-2	0-4	11	5	0	4
Rich	3-5	1-2	1-4	0-3	8	1	0	0
Mims	0-1	0-0	0-0	0-2	0	0	0	0
Allen	0-0	0-0	0-0	0-0	0	1	0	0
Breeden	1-1	0-0	1-2	1-0	3	1	0	2
Wilson	4-6	3-5	2-2	0-2	13	0	0	0
Romero	3-3	0-0	3-4	0-3	9	1	0	2
Echefu	2-6	0-1	1-2	0-0	5	0	0	1
Totals	24-49	6-17	12-22	3-20	66	13	1	11
	(49.0%)	(35.3%)	(54.5%)					

Florida

Player	FGM-A	3FGM-A	FTM-A	O-D REB	TP	A	BLK	S
Brewer	3-10	0-2	7-10	1-5	13	6	2	2
Noah	1-3	0-0	1-2	0-2	3	1	2	1
Horford	4-8	0-0	6-10	3-6	14	1	1	1
Green	0-2	0-2	15-16	0-4	15	4	0	0
Humphrey	4-7	3-5	0-0	0-2	11	1	0	2
Moss	1-2	0-0	1-1	1-1	3	0	0	0
Hodge	3-6	2-5	2-4	0-1	10	1	0	0
Richard	2-2	0-0	1-2	0-1	5	0	0	0
Huertas	0-0	0-0	0-0	0-0	0	0	0	0
Totals	18-40	5-14	33-45	5-22	74	14	5	6
	(45.0%)	(35.7%)	(73.3%)					

#11 TAUREAN GREEN

By Kevin Brockway, *Sun sports writer*

When Taurean Green found out the starting Florida point guard job was his to lose this past summer, he went to the videotape, critiquing the little things he did wrong in his freshman season.

What Green observed was a player going too fast for his own good.

"I was in a rush last year," Green said. "I was in a hurry."

The game slowed down for Green in time as a sophomore, where he is off to a confident beginning as the starting point guard at Florida this season.

"He's running the offense like a champion," Florida senior forward Adrian Moss said. "He always gets us in the offense. And everything that needs to be done, he gets done."

For Green, the education began last year as the understudy to two-time, All-Southeastern Conference point guard Anthony Roberson. Green credited Roberson for his development as a freshman. The two went head-to-head in practice.

"He taught me a lot just learning from him in game situations, also in practice, what passes I could get away with and what passes I couldn't make," Green said. "It's carried over to this season. I'm still learning, but I'm just trying to learn from every game and try to get better."

Roberson left for the NBA as an underclassman, opening the door for Green to join classmates Corey Brewer and Al Horford in the starting lineup. Green has managed to handle the pressure of the most important position on the court by keeping his teammates involved while supplying his own offense when needed.

In back-to-back wins against Wake Forest and Syracuse, it was at the three-point line, where Green shot a combined 10-for-17 in posting back-to-back 23-point games. Against Florida State and Alabama Stat0e, it was at the foul line, where Green has made 24 straight and 25 of his last 26.

Florida coach Billy Donovan said he hasn't been surprised with Green's offense. As a high-school senior, Green posted two 50-plus point games at Cardinal Gibbons High in Fort Lauderdale.

"Right now, anyone could really be leading our team in scoring," Donovan said. "If you look at why Taurean is leading our team now it's because he's shot the ball well from the three-point line and has gotten to the free throw line."

"I think I'm getting better at that," Green said. "It's just taking what the defense gives you. They are pressuring me. You just have to keep the defense honest and go past them a couple of times and get in the lane and create for my offense."

It's been a special start to the season for Green, whose father, former NBA forward Sidney Green, was able to watch him in his breakout performance in New York City. Green dedicated his MVP performance to his late grandmother, Sidney's mother, who died last January and had always wanted to see her grandson play at Madison Square Garden.

Sidney, an Indiana assistant coach, first enrolled Taurean in Florida summer basketball camps when he was a 5-foot-8 eighth-grader. Donovan saw potential, but was waiting for Green to grow a couple of inches.

"The biggest thing with Taurean his freshman and sophomore year is would he get taller, would he get stronger, would he grow, would he develop," Donovan said. "I was impressed with him after his sophomore year in camp, just his mind, his understanding, and his feel for the game. I'm sure Sidney played a major role in that."

Now, as a sophomore in college, Green is making another leap, one he hopes will carry him as the starting point guard through the rest of his college career.

"Yeah, I'd like it to be that way," Green said. "Be here all four years and have fun every year."

Name: Taurean Green
Hometown: Boca Raton, FL
Attended: Cardinal Gibbons H.S.
Year: Sophomore
Major: Social and Behavioral Sciences
Position: Guard
Height: 6-feet
Weight: 177 pounds

MAGNIFICENT 11

By KEVIN BROCKWAY, *Sun sports writer*

Down the stretch, Florida coach Billy Donovan asked his weary team if they wanted to pack in a zone or play man-to-man defense.

The collective response—man defense.

With huge stops late, No. 5 Florida cemented its best start in school history, beating pesky Miami 77-67 to avenge a loss at the O'Connell Center a season ago. At 11-0, Florida eclipsed the 1951-52 team, the last to start a season with 10 straight wins.

"They'll always be in the record books," Donovan said. "It's something nice that they can look back on. But to me, it's what you do with this going forward."

In front of a frenzied half-Gator, half-Hurricane crowd at the sold-out BankUnited Center, Florida rallied from down nine points in the first half and kept its composure late by scoring inside and holding the Hurricanes scoreless in the final 2:10. Florida (11-0) closed the game with a 10-0 run. Al Horford started it with a bank shot that broke a 67-67 tie. It ended with six straight free throws from Horford, Corey Brewer and Taurean Green.

Joakim Noah led Florida with 18 points and 6 blocks, including a big one against Miami center Anthony King with 59 seconds left.

"If you want to win games, you have to make stops," Noah said. "We want to win games, so we have to make stops."

Lee Humphrey pounced on the loose ball in a scramble on the floor, then called time out to ensure Florida retained possession.

Humphrey tied a career high with 15 points for the Gators, going 5-of-6 from three-point range. Brewer chipped in 13 despite going 2-of-12 from the floor.

"It means a lot, after what we did last year," Brewer said. "Plus, we beat all the Florida schools. We can say that we're the Florida champions."

OPPOSITE PAGE: Joakim Noah, who led the Gators with 18 points, slams home a mighty dunk. *AP/WWP*

It didn't look that way early. Florida came out sluggish and Miami pounced, jumping to a 15-8 lead after the Gators settled for shots from the perimeter instead of taking the ball inside. Miami's guards scored all 15 points during the early run.

"We had some good looks that we didn't hit early, and for the first time, I think it affected us on the defensive end," Donovan said. "Our intensity lessened. I just told our guys, 'Look, we've never worried about scoring. Let's just focus on the defensive end and try to get out on the break.'"

Guillermo Diaz led the Hurricanes (6-5) with 25 points on 8-of-18 shooting. Anthony Harris added 16, and Robert Hite scored 12, as Miami relied on its guards for scoring throughout.

Diaz eclipsed the 20-point mark for the eighth time against his last 11 ranked opponents.

"It was a high-level ballgame," Miami coach Frank Haith said. "We're disappointed with the outcome. Their big guys had us down at the end, outscoring us 24-8 in the paint. We did a good job with their post guys until the final five minutes of the game."

Said Diaz: "We fought hard. We just didn't execute at the end."

Miami extended its lead to 31-22 on three free throws by Harris after he was fouled by Green with 1:52 remaining. But Florida closed the half with an unlikely 11-2 run to tie the game. Green pulled Florida within 33-28 with a three-pointer at the 1:12 mark. Freshman David Huertas followed with a

lay-up and, in the closing seconds, Brewer was fouled by Harris as he was about to heave the desperation three-pointer from 35 feet.

Brewer made all three free throws with 0.9 seconds left, tying the score at 33 at halftime. At that point, Florida felt good about its chances.

"We knew we had it," Brewer said.

"I think our guys learned something about themselves tonight," Donovan said. "They learned that they can come back on the road in front of a hostile crowd. It wasn't a perfect game. There are a lot of things that we can work on going forward."

	1st	2nd	Total
Florida	33	44	77
Miami	33	34	67

Florida

Player	FGM-A	3FGM-A	FTM-A	O-D REB	TP	A	BLK	S
Brewer	2-12	0-4	9-12	2-2	13	5	0	2
Noah	5-9	0-0	8-11	4-4	18	2	6	1
Horford	1-4	0-0	4-6	1-6	6	0	3	1
Green	3-11	3-7	2-2	0-3	11	4	0	1
Humphrey	5-6	5-6	0-0	0-3	15	1	0	0
Moss	2-3	0-0	0-0	0-0	4	1	0	0
Hodge	1-6	0-2	0-0	0-1	2	0	0	2
Richard	2-3	0-0	2-2	6-1	6	1	1	0
Huertas	1-3	0-2	0-0	1-1	2	0	0	0
Totals	22-57 (38.6%)	8-21 (38.1%)	25-33 (75.8%)	14-21	77	14	10	7

Miami

Player	FGM-A	3FGM-A	FTM-A	O-D REB	TP	A	TO	BLK	S
Graham	0-3	0-0	2-4	1-2	2	0		2	1
King	1-6	0-0	2-4	1-7	4	1		3	1
Harris	4-7	1-1	7-7	0-1	16	1		0	2
Diaz	8-18	3-6	6-7	0-4	25	2		1	0
Hite	4-8	2-4	2-2	2-2	12	0		0	2
Hamilton	0-2	0-0	0-2	3-4	0	0		1	1
Wilkins	1-2	0-0	1-1	0-1	3	0		1	0
Clemente	1-4	0-2	1-3	2-1	3	2		0	0
Thomas	1-2	0-0	0-0	2-0	2	0		0	0
Totals	20-52 (38.5%)	6-13 (46.2%)	21-30 (70.0%)	11-22	67	6		8	7

GATORS GRITTY IN HISTORIC WIN

By KEVIN BROCKWAY, *Sun sports writer*

With half his teammates sick and the other half in foul trouble, Florida starting point guard Taurean Green at one point in the first half asked coach Billy Donovan if he was taking too many shots.

"I told Taurean, 'Who else is going to take them?'" Donovan said.

On a night when Green hoisted up an uncharacteristic 18 attempts, No. 2 Florida survived some shaky first-half stretches to beat Mississippi State 75-60 in a game with some chippy, mouthy moments.

Green finished with a team-high 20 points, including a deep three-pointer that sealed the game late. Florida (15-0, 2-0 SEC) broke a school record for consecutive wins in a game that Donovan described as a humbling experience.

Tensions boiled over during a postgame handshake in a confrontation between Florida forward Chris Richard and Mississippi State freshman Jamont Gordon that involved some pushing and shoving. Gordon, who led the Bulldogs with 17 points, had traded some verbal barbs with Green during the course of the game.

"He tried to take a swing at me," Gordon said. "He came really close to hitting me. If he would have hit me, we would have fought."

"It's a competitive basketball game and everyone is out there playing hard," said senior forward Adrian Moss. "For a freshman to go at Chris is surprising. He's a pretty big dude."

Richard (2 points, 5 rebounds) and Moss (8 points, 3 rebounds) provided lifts off the bench for Florida, which had to deal with one starting for-

OPPOSITE PAGE: Taurean Green scrambles for a loose ball with Mississippi State's Dietric Slater.
Michael C. Weimar/The Gainesville Sun

"You can call it iffy. I call it a win. It's an SEC win. They're all important."

—Adrian Moss
Florida forward

ward sick and the other in foul trouble. Al Horford had missed the previous two practices with strep throat and was on antibiotics. Brewer, who added 18 points, picked up two early fouls and sat the final 9:56 of the first half.

Lee Humphrey also picked up his second foul with 10:16 left in the first half. With both Humphrey and Brewer on the bench, an early 26-12 Florida lead nearly vanished. Mississippi State went on a 13-0 run, frustrating Florida into four turnovers and seven straight missed shots during a 5:56 scoreless stretch.

Florida was forced to rely on freshman guards Walter Hodge and David Huertas for extended minutes. Huertas also had been suffering a bad case of strep and nearly fumbled the ball out of bounds in one of his few touches when he was on the floor.

"We didn't want to put David into the game, but we didn't have much of a choice," Donovan

LEFT: Under heavy pressure, Al Horford looks to pass between two Bulldogs defenders.
Michael C. Weimar/The Gainesville Sun

said. "Anthony (associate coach Anthony Grant) was out of eligibility."

Humphrey eventually checked back into the game at the 5:36 mark, and the run ended when Horford made one of two free throws to put Florida up 27-25. Green followed with a pretty, driving lay-up in the lane.

Florida extended its lead to 32-27 when a Green steal set up a Hodge lay-up in transition. But Mississippi State followed with a lay-in by Sharpe and a three-pointer by Reginald Delk with 25.7 seconds remaining to tie the score at 32.

Green, with 8.7 seconds remaining, sank an open three-pointer from the top of the arc to put Florida up 35-32 at halftime.

Florida, which came into the game leading the NCAA in assists at 20.1 per game, had just three in first half.

"You can't get many assists if you don't shoot the ball well," Donovan said. "I thought our player movement in the first half at times was poor."

"For some reason, we weren't moving the ball well," Green said. "We stressed that at halftime. We were able to get Corey and Lee back into the flow."

In the second half, Florida got back out on the break, eventually building a comfortable lead behind the shooting of Humphrey and some electric plays from Brewer. An alley-oop from Brewer to Green extended Florida's lead to 45-36. It was 60-40 after two Green free throws with 11:12 remaining.

From there, Florida worked the shot clock. Two three pointers from Green as the shot clock wound down staved off some runs that were sparked by the driving Gordon, who scored 12 of his 17 in the second half.

Mississippi State played without leading scorer Jamall Edmondson, who sat out his third straight game with a pulled groin. Without their best ball handler, the Bulldogs (11-4, 1-1 SEC) couldn't overcome 24 turnovers.

"I was proud of our team's effort," Mississippi State coach Rick Stansbury said. "The Florida basketball team presents many problems."

That Florida survived some anxious moments against Mississippi State was a sign of some resolve.

"You can call it iffy," Moss said. "I call it a win. It's an SEC win. They're all important."

		1st	2nd	Total
Mississippi State		32	28	60
Florida		35	40	75

Mississippi State

Name	FGM-A	3FGM-A	FTM-A	O-D REB	TP	A	BLK	S
Rhodes	6-11	0-0	0-1	2-7	12	0	2	1
Gordon	6-12	0-1	5-8	2-5	17	7	0	0
Morgan	2-3	0-0	2-5	3-0	6	0	1	3
Slater	5-9	0-1	1-1	0-2	11	0	1	1
Delk, Re	2-6	2-4	0-0	0-3	6	1	0	2
Delk, Ri	0-0	0-0	0-0	0-0	0	0	0	0
Houston	0-4	0-1	0-0	0-1	0	0	0	1
Boler	0-0	0-0	0-0	0-0	0	0	0	0
Stelmach	1-2	0-1	0-2	1-1	2	0	0	0
Sharpe	2-6	0-0	2-2	4-3	6	1	1	0
Totals	24-53	2-8	10-19	12-22	60	9	5	8
	(45.3%)	(25.0%)	(52.6%)					

Florida

Player	FGM-A	3FGM-A	FTM-A	O-D REF	TP	A	BLK	S
Brewer	4-11	0-3	10-13	1-3	18	3	1	1
Noah	1-3	0-0	3-4	2-5	5	1	3	2
Horford	3-5	0-0	1-4	1-1	7	0	1	1
Green	6-18	5-11	3-4	1-1	20	5	0	3
Humphrey	5-7	3-5	0-0	1-2	13	0	0	2
Moss	3-4	0-1	2-3	2-1	8	1	0	1
Hodge	1-5	0-2	0-0	0-3	2	1	0	2
Richard	1-2	0-0	0-0	3-2	2	1	1	1
Huertas	0-0	0-0	0-0	0-0	0	0	0	0
Totals	24-55	8-22	19-28	11-18	75	12	6	13
	(43.6%)	(36.4%)	(67.9%)					

#13 JOAKIM NOAH

By Kevin Brockway, *Sun sports writer*

The epiphany came in a Nashville, Tennessee, hotel room, shortly after Florida's first-round NCAA Tournament win against Ohio University.

Joakim Noah was with Florida coach Billy Donovan, in part to help scout second-round opponent Villanova and in part to lobby for some playing time after not appearing in the Ohio game.

"He was a kid at the end of last year that was completely devastated," Donovan said. "He was very, emotional. He was so competitive and passionate and wanted to play."

"It's still a painful memory," Noah said. "But it's definitely an experience that's going to help me."

Spurred by the limited playing time as a freshman, Noah was in the weight room the morning after the season ended, working out with assistant coach Larry Shyatt.

The message Donovan provided in the hotel-room summit was patience.

"I told Jo, 'This season is going to come to an end.'" Donovan said. "David Lee is going to be gone. It's not about right now. Right now it's about you learning. It's not about you getting playing time.

"Ever since that talk his focus is totally changed because he realizes you know what, I'm going to be relied upon this year. I wasn't last year, and I don't want to let my teammates and the coaches down. So he's come really, really focused. He's gotten better. He had a really good off-season."

Noah arrived on campus this semester at the same 227 pounds he was as a freshman. But his body shape was different. More strength was packed into his chest and shoulders.

"I definitely feel good physically and mentally," Noah said. "I feel good for the season to start."

Mentally, Noah was able to refresh by spending a month in Africa with his father and grandfather. The trip to Cameroon gave Noah time to reflect on his freshman season.

"I didn't really focus on basketball, but I knew as soon I was going to come back and step on this campus I would give 150 percent into becoming better and getting ready for the season," Noah said.

What Noah noticed in Cameroon was that not much had changed in his father and grandfather's native country since he last visited six years ago.

"Poverty has really struck over there but the people are just really happy," Noah said. "There's no hunger. It's just a different atmosphere.

"We were having a game and there must have been like 25 guys on the court. Some guy actually called offsides on me and it was like, 'This isn't soccer man, it's basketball.'"

There were plenty of long conversations with his grandfather, a former French national soccer player, and his father, former French Open tennis champion Yannick Noah.

"They just told me too keep working," Noah said. "The people who work the hardest are the ones who usually make it, you know, at this level. You usually have a thousand people at your level, and you have to have your goals straight, and know what you want in life. If you're lucky, you'll get them."

Noah came into the fall determined to prove he deserved more playing time.

"Jo is a worker," Donovan said. "He's one of the first guys in the gym every day and one of the last ones to leave. He has a very, very unique competitiveness and drive about him, he's very internally driven.

"The emotion that he plays with, he does it every day in practice. That's the thing that's been encouraging."

Name: Joakim Noah
Hometown: New York, NY
Attended: Lawrenceville Prep (NJ)
Year: Sophomore
Major: Social and Behavioral Sciences
Position: Forward/Center
Height: 6-foot-11
Weight: 227 pounds

Tracy Wilcox/The Gainesville Sun

JANUARY 25, 2006

COLONIAL CENTER, COLUMBIA, SOUTH CAROLINA

ROAD WOES

By **KEVIN BROCKWAY,** *Sun sports writer*

Five days ago Florida was considered for the top spot in the nation. Today, the Gators find themselves tied for second in the Southeastern Conference's East division.

In an example of how quickly things can change in college basketball, No. 5 Florida (17-2, 3-2 SEC) struggled mightily in a 68-62 loss at South Carolina. Unlike the Tennessee loss that dropped Florida from the unbeaten ranks, Florida played the Gamecocks with surprisingly little energy or focus.

The players admitted as much afterward.

"We've just got to start playing basketball the way we know how to play," said sophomore forward Corey Brewer. "We're playing too pretty right now. We've got to get back to being gritty.

"We're not hitting people in the mouth. We're letting other people hit us in the mouth."

Florida put together a flurry of four straight three-pointers late—three by Taurean Green and one by Walter Hodge—that pulled the Gators with-

in 65-60 with 48.5 seconds left. But South Carolina guard Tarence Kinsey hit two free throws late and made a game-clinching steal against Green as the clock wound down.

About the only drama that remained late was whether students would storm the court. A few tried, but a security presence, that included erecting a rope around the perimeter of the court, kept fans at bay.

Though Florida was only out-rebounded 32-31, South Carolina grabbed 14 offensive rebounds. Turnovers were another problem. Florida committed 17, including 10 in the first half.

Florida, hailed as one of the best pass-and-catch teams by South Carolina coach Dave Odom before the game, had trouble with the catch part in trying to get the ball inside.

OPPOSITE PAGE: Walter Hodge (15) battles South Carolina's Tre Kelley for a loose ball in front of Rocky Trice (10). *AP/WWP*

"The level of focus they needed to have wasn't there," Florida coach Billy Donovan said. "I have to take responsibility for it, and we all have to take responsibility for it."

Joakim Noah finished with his first career double-double at Florida, with 12 points and 13 rebounds. Green led Florida in scoring with 17 points and Hodge added 10 points off the bench.

"I could see it before the game, in the hotel, while we traveled," Noah said. "We didn't come out with that edge. We have to find that edge and get it back."

Brewer started, but clearly wasn't himself. Brewer, who suffered a lateral right ankle sprain that he played through against Tennessee, finished with 7 points and two assists and was missing the lift that's vital to his game.

An example of Brewer's inability to get off the floor came after a steal. He drove in for a break-away lay-up but couldn't convert. Brewer was bailed out by a phantom foul call against South Carolina guard Tre Kelley.

With Brewer hobbled, Florida attempted to establish an inside presence early. Florida actually jumped to an early 13-4 lead but couldn't sustain it. Renaldo Balkman gave South Carolina a lift, scoring three baskets during an 8-0 run. The last, a lay-up around Florida forward Chris Richard, gave the Gamecocks their first lead, 16-15.

South Carolina didn't trail the rest of the way, leading 29-23 at halftime and by as many as 15 in the second half until a late Florida charge.

Kinsey, a Tampa native, led South Carolina with 19 points. Balkman scored 14 off the bench to help South Carolina (11-8, 2-4) snap a nine-game losing streak against Florida.

"I'm sure there'll be some type of argument from somebody, but I can't think of a team that needed a win more than ours did anywhere in the country," Odom said.

"We've been playing soft," Noah said. "We've been listening to all the hype. We've got to get back to playing the kind of basketball we were when we started the season."

OPPOSITE PAGE: Joakim Noah goes up for a block on Brandon Wallace's shot. *AP/WWP*

	1st	2nd	Total
Florida	23	39	62
South Carolina	29	39	68

Florida

Player	FGM-A	3FGM-A	FTM-A	O-D REB	TP	A	BLK	S
Brewer	2-7	1-5	2-2	0-1	7	2	0	1
Noah	4-6	0-0	4-4	1-12	12	1	1	0
Horford	3-8	0-0	0-0	3-6	6	0	1	1
Green	5-12	3-6	4-4	0-2	17	7	0	0
Humphrey	2-6	2-6	0-0	0-2	6	0	0	1
Moss	0-0	0-0	0-0	0-0	0	0	0	0
Hodge	4-4	2-2	0-0	0-0	10	1	0	2
Richard	2-2	0-0	0-0	1-2	4	0	0	0
Huertas	0-0	0-0	0-0	0-0	0	0	0	0
Totals	22-45 (48.9%)	8-21 (38.1%)	10-10 (100 %)	5-25	62	11	2	5

South Carolina

Player	FGM-A	3FGM-A	FTM-A	O-D REB	TP	A	BLK	S
Day	1-8	1-7	1-2	1-3	4	0	0	1
Wallace	2-3	0-1	0-0	1-1	4	1	0	1
Tisby	3-9	0-0	3-6	3-2	9	0	3	2
Kelley	3-9	0-3	2-6	2-3	8	8	0	1
Kinsey	5-13	3-4	6-8	2-2	19	2	1	1
McDowell	1-3	1-3	0-0	0-0	3	1	0	0
Trice	3-5	1-2	0-0	1-2	7	1	0	1
Balkman	6-7	0-0	2-4	2-4	14	2	0	3
Totals	24-57 (42.1%)	6-20 (30.0%)	14-26 (53.8%)	12-17	68	15	4	10

SWAGGER'S BACK

By KEVIN BROCKWAY, *Sun sports writer*

They were all smiles and raised fists and chest-bumps heading into the locker room.

In front of a national audience, Florida regained some of its lost swagger, beating former nemesis Kentucky 95-80 before a record 12,606 at the O'Connell Center.

Taurean Green and Joakim Noah had career highs in scoring, sparking the Florida onslaught. Green finished with 29 points and 9 assists, often feeding Noah either inside or as he was streaking on the break. Noah had 26 points, scoring six of his baskets on dunks, and had 7 rebounds.

Florida won its third straight against Kentucky for the first time since 1984-85, tilting the tables on a Kentucky eight-game winning streak that had preceded the Gators' recent run.

"It's just one game," Green said. "We're 1-0 against Kentucky, that's the way we look at it. Last season was last season. We know we have to play them at least one more time, so we have to be ready when we see them again."

After a tight first half, Florida was able to run away from the Wildcats in the second, scoring more than 90 points for the first time since its January 18 win against Savannah State.

"They key was our defense in the second half," Green said. "We were able to force them into bad shots and get baskets in transition."

The win also moved Florida (20-2, 6-2 SEC) into sole possession of second place in the SEC East, a game behind 7-1 Tennessee. Florida reached 20 wins for an eighth straight season under coach Billy Donovan.

Florida's 95 points were the most against Kentucky at home since 1968.

Rajon Rondo led Kentucky (15-7, 5-3) with 22 points, with fellow sophomore guard Joe Crawford

---

OPPOSITE PAGE: Taurean Green pushes the ball up-court against Kentucky. *Tracy Wilcox/The Gainesville Sun*

chipping in 19. Kentucky center Randolph Morris scored 10 of his 14 points in the first half.

Sophomore forward Corey Brewer started and junior guard Lee Humphrey played, marked improvements from the more dire projections Florida coach Billy Donovan gave Thursday. Their presence gave the Gators a lift. Brewer, in his first start since January 25 at South Carolina, played his best game since spraining his right ankle two weeks ago against Tennessee, finishing with 16 points, 4 rebounds and 4 assists.

"I was able to play my game," Brewer said. "My ankle wasn't bothering me when I woke up. I wasn't stiff, wasn't sore. I felt back to being myself out there."

With Brewer near 100 percent, Florida was able to get back to the running, pressing style that had sparked it to a school-record 17-game winning streak to start the season.

Down by six early in the second half, Florida responded with a game-altering 18-1 run. Brewer began it with two free throws, followed by a Green three-pointer and a Horford lay-in to put Florida back in the lead, 46-45. After a Green 14-foot jumper, Green again found Noah on an alley-oop inbounds play. Noah leaped from the three-quarters mark from the free throw line for the dunk, sending the sold-out O'Connell Center crowd into a frenzy.

From there, Florida continued to pile on the points, with Noah tipping in a Green miss and Green sinking another 14-footer. After a Crawford free throw pulled Kentucky within 54-46, Green answered with another three, putting Florida up 57-46.

The first matchup between the two schools since Florida's 70-53 win in the SEC Tournament finals lived up to the pregame buildup early. With ESPN's *College GameDay* crew on hand, both teams maintained a fast pace throughout, mixing crisp plays with finishes on the break.

Florida began with the press, forcing turnovers on Kentucky's first two possessions. Green hit Florida's first shot, a 14-foot jumper. Noah got into the offensive flow early, scoring three of his first four baskets on dunks off assists.

ABOVE: Soaring over teammate Walter Hodge (15), Joakim Noah leaps to block Kentucky's Rajon Rondo. *Tracy Wilcox/The Gainesville Sun*
OPPOSITE PAGE: Al Horford lays up a shot around Wildcat forward Bobby Perry. *Tracy Wilcox/The Gainesville Sun*

Though Brewer didn't score early, he was active driving to the basket, feeding Noah and Chris Richard for early baskets.

Humphrey checked in at the 14:23 mark and showed signs of rust, launching an air ball in his first three-point attempt. On defense, Humphrey responded well after having early problems staying with Rondo.

Neither team built a lead of more than 4 points in the first half until a three-pointer from Kentucky reserve forward Sheray Thomas put the Wildcats up 39-34 with 2:07 left. Florida responded by driving inside, drawing fouls on Kentucky backup center Lukasz Orbzut on three straight possessions. Green made 3 of 4 free throws and Richard made two free throws with 42.2 seconds left to tie the score at 39.

Florida had a chance for the last shot of the half, but Noah couldn't corral a missed three-point attempt from Rekalin Sims, fumbling the ball out of bounds with 16.3 seconds left. The Wildcats then held for the last shot, with Crawford sinking a soft jumper in the lane before time expired to put Kentucky ahead 41-39 at halftime.

Still, Florida felt good about itself going into the half because of the way it moved the basketball. The Gators finished with 20 assists.

"We just worked off each other," Green said. "We got back to the style that we like to play."

	1st	2nd	Total
Kentucky	41	39	80
Florida	39	56	95

Kentucky

Player	FGM-A	3FGM-A	FTM-A	O-D REB	TP	A	BLK	S
Perry	2-4	2-2	0-0	0-0	6	0	0	0
Morris	6-8	0-0	2-2	1-3	14	6	1	1
Rondo	8-13	3-4	3-5	0-4	22	0	0	5
Sparks	2-11	1-6	0-0	0-1	5	9	0	1
Crawford	5-16	2-8	7-8	4-6	19	0	0	0
Stockton	0-0	0-0	0-0	0-0	0	0	0	0
Moss	0-2	0-1	0-0	1-1	0	0	0	1
Bradley	2-7	1-4	2-2	1-0	7	0	0	0
Obrzut	0-0	0-0	0-0	0-1	0	0	0	0
LeMaster	0-0	0-0	0-0	0-0	0	0	0	0
Thomas	2-4	1-2	2-4	2-2	7	0	0	0
Sims	0-1	0-1	0-0	0-0	0	0	0	0
Carter	0-1	0-0	0-0	0-1	0	0	0	0
Totals	27-67 (40.3%)	10-28 (35.7%)	16-21 (76.2%)	9-19	80	15	1	8

Florida

Player	FGM-A	3FGM-A	FTM-A	O-D REB	TP	A	BLK	S
Brewer	3-9	1-4	9-10	1-3	16	4	0	2
Noah	11-13	0-0	4-6	2-6	26	2	3	1
Horford	3-3	0-0	5-7	2-9	11	1	3	0
Green	8-14	3-7	10-12	0-4	29	9	1	3
Hodge	0-4	0-1	0-0	0-2	0	1	0	1
Swanson	0-0	0-0	0-0	0-0	0	0	0	0
Moss	0-0	0-0	0-0	0-0	0	0	0	0
Humphrey	0-1	0-1	0-0	0-0	0	2	0	1
Berry	0-0	0-0	0-0	0-0	0	0	0	0
Tyler	0-0	0-0	0-0	0-0	0	0	0	0
Richard	4-5	0-0	2-2	0-1	10	1	0	0
Huertas	1-3	1-2	0-0	0-1	3	0	0	0
Totals	30-52 (57.7%)	5-15 (33.3%)	30-37 (81.1%)	5-26	95	20	7	8

#42 AL HORFORD

By Kevin Brockway, *Sun sports writer*

After his surprise freshman year, Florida forward Al Horford returned to Grande Ledge, Michigan, over the summer for a few weeks of rest and catching up with family.

If Horford needed any extra motivation heading into his sophomore season, he gained it from playing pickup games against Michigan State players who were coming off a trip to the Final Four the April before.

"No doubt," Horford said. "Those guys had a great team last year."

By way of Michigan and the Dominican Republic, the soft-spoken Horford let his play inside do the talking last season. Now as a sophomore, Horford will be asked to lead as well as produce.

"Al's not going to say a lot," Florida coach Billy Donovan said. "When he steps across the lines he understands it's serious. There's not a whole lot of laughing and joking around with him. He pays attention to detail. He's just a great guy to coach because he cares so much."

Horford signaled his arrival in December 2004, when he replaced senior Adrian Moss as Florida's starting center after Moss went down with disc problems in his back.

"I'm pleased with his energy," Donovan said. "The biggest thing that he's trying to do is become a little bit more consistent in scoring around the basket when he catches it. But in terms of him blocking shots, rebounding, the way that he has played so far has been positive."

Some added strength has helped. The 6-foot-8 Horford gained 17 pounds during the offseason, much of it in his upper body. At a broad-shouldered 250, Horford appears ready to endure the banging he will take as Florida's first option in the post this season.

"I think I have a little more power and more strength in my legs," Horford said. "I feel more confident because I'm stronger."

More will be asked of him. Gone is senior forward David Lee, who drew much of the attention from defenses in the post. Horford averaged 5.6 points as a freshman, but his scoring output dipped late in the season as defenses paid more attention to him.

"You always have a big benefit on having a good player like David," Horford said. "This year is going to be a lot different. I really don't know what I'm going to step into. But I feel like I have good teammates around me that are going to help me throughout that."

Indeed, Horford and Lee were different players, which is why they complemented each other so well when they started together.

"He's a different type of player than David," Florida assistant coach Anthony Grant said. "David's biggest asset was his junior year (when) he was the second-leading assist guy, last year he was second or third in assists. David could beat you with his passing and his scoring, where I think Al's biggest assets are his shot-blocking, his rebounding and his ability to score with the back to the basket. So you're talking about different players. We're going to try to implement a system that's going to play to his strengths."

Nor does Horford feel pressure to score.

"I'm just going with whatever coach is telling me to go," Horford said. "I'm working within the offensive framework. Whatever he wants me to do, I'm going to do."

Still, Horford spent much of the offseason perfecting his post moves. Moss, who matches up with Horford in practice, has noticed a difference between last season and this season.

"They are a lot more polished," Moss said. "He's finishing better with his left and right. He just has a better understanding of angles and when to use the right move."

Moss believes that Horford could end his sophomore year as the best big man in the SEC this season.

"Why not?" Moss asked. "Al always steps up to every challenge, as he did last year. Al is going to be just fine."

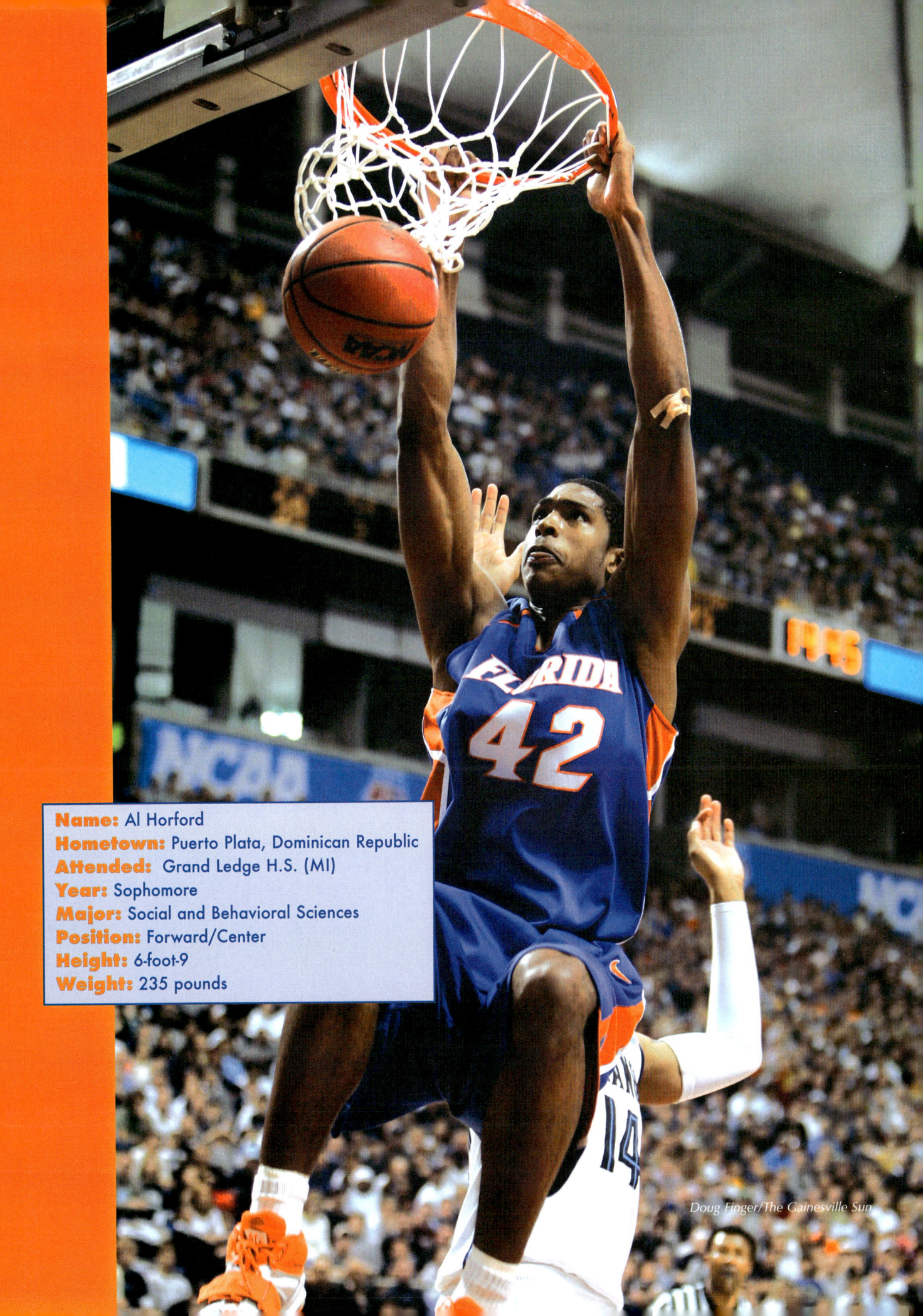

Name: Al Horford
Hometown: Puerto Plata, Dominican Republic
Attended: Grand Ledge H.S. (MI)
Year: Sophomore
Major: Social and Behavioral Sciences
Position: Forward/Center
Height: 6-foot-9
Weight: 235 pounds

Doug Finger/The Gainesville Sun

MUCH-NEEDED VICTORY

By PAT DOOLEY, *Sun sports writer*

It was all about adjustments. Florida adjusted its defense, adjusted to some bizarre no-calls, adjusted to the league's biggest body down low.

But more than anything, the Gators adjusted their attitudes for this game with LSU.

And the result was the biggest win of the season for Florida.

They couldn't afford another loss at home. Instead, they beat the best team in the conference.

"You had to be on edge the whole game out there," center Al Horford said. "If you don't against a team like LSU, they'll dunk on your head."

It was Horford who made one of the big adjustments of the game, finally figuring out how to handle Glen "Big Baby" Davis, the biggest man to ever wear tights on a basketball court and not have to worry about anyone making fun of him.

At the half, Florida was getting killed on the boards again, and no matter how loudly the O-Dome fans were booing the officials, they knew in their hearts that if the Gators lost this game it would be the same old problem—hitting the glass.

But Horford realized that it wasn't getting the rebounds that was as important as not letting his man get the missed shots. Florida ended up outrebounding the Tigers by seven in the second half.

OPPOSITE PAGE: Making a strong move against LSU's Glen "Big Baby" Davis, Al Horford drives to the hoop. Horford had 16 points against the Tigers. *Tracy Wilcox/The Gainesville Sun*

FEBRUARY 11, 2006

"You're not going to box him out," Florida coach Billy Donovan said. "He is, in our league, Shaquille O'Neal."

Davis wore the scars of an intense game in the locker room—a sore shoulder and a cut over his right eye—and the kind of line that illustrated how well Florida played against him—11 missed shots and four turnovers.

He did score 16 points and grab 15 rebounds, but even John Brady felt that Florida's big guys outplayed his.

"Their inside was better than ours," he said.

That's because Horford and Joakim Noah combined for 32 points, 13 rebounds and six blocked shots. Florida had to get that kind of performance in a game it had to have.

But it was more than winning the low post. The Gators took away Darrel Mitchell's three-point shot one game after he drilled a three to give LSU a win over Arkansas. They gave the point guard different looks on defense, disrupting LSU's offensive flow.

And they wore the depth-challenged Tigers out with the press and fast breaks and a helter-skelter style of play.

More than anything, Florida played like Florida should have played in the loss to South Carolina. The sandwich game of this three-game home stand left the Gators hungry.

"It's hard when everyone on campus is telling you how good you are," Noah said of the days following the Kentucky win. "My dad told me that it's one thing to go the gym and everybody is telling you on the way there how good you are. But when nobody is talking to you, you still have to go to work.

"We did what we had to do." They had to get this one. It was so important on so many levels—Southeastern Conference standings, SEC seed, NCAA seed, psyche and swagger.

LEFT: Joakim Noah rips down a defensive rebound. Noah led the Gators in rebounding with nine on the night.

Tracy Wilcox/The Gainesville Sun

ABOVE: Corey Brewer applies defensive pressure to his LSU man. *Tracy Wilcox/The Gainesville Sun*

	1st	2nd	Total
LSU	37	25	62
Florida	37	34	71

LSU

Player	FGM-A	3FGM-A	FTM-A	O-D REF	TP	A	BLK	S
Davis	5-16	0-0	6-12	9-6	16	0	0	0
Mitchell, T	5-11	0-3	4-4	2-1	14	1	1	1
Thomas	1-3	0-0	0-0	1-3	2	0	0	0
Temple	1-2	1-2	0-1	0-3	3	2	1	1
Mitchell, D	5-16	1-6	0-0	0-3	11	4	0	1
Voogd	0-0	0-0	0-0	0-0	0	3	0	0
Rolle	2-4	0-0	2-2	1-2	6	0	0	1
Lazare	5-8	0-0	0-0	1-2	10	1	0	0
Totals	24-60	2-11	12-19	14-20	62	11	2	4
	(40.0%)	(18.2%)	(63.2%)					

Florida

Player	FGM-A	3FGM-A	FTM-A	O-D REB	TP	A	BLK	S
Brewer	1-7	0-2	4-4	1-3	6	2	0	1
Noah	6-11	0-0	4-6	3-6	16	1	2	0
Horford	8-11	0-0	0-2	1-3	16	2	4	1
Green	1-9	1-6	0-1	2-3	3	7	0	1
Hodge	3-3	0-0	1-1	0-0	7	1	0	2
Moss	1-3	0-0	2-4	1-2	4	0	0	0
Humphrey	5-7	3-4	0-0	0-2	13	2	0	0
Richard	3-5	0-0	0-0	0-1	6	0	0	0
Huertas	0-2	0-1	0-0	2-0	0	1	0	0
Totals	28-58	4-13	11-18	10-20	71	16	6	5
	(48.3%)	(30.8%)	(61.1%)					

And they needed it because they needed a signature win in what has been a remarkable season. Beating Kentucky is always beating Kentucky, but beating LSU means a lot more around the nation and to the RPI.

To win a game like Saturday's, you have to know it's not going to be easy or pretty. You can't be bothered by bad breaks, bad calls, bad shots or bad mistakes. Or by bad games like the one they played against South Carolina.

"I'm always telling our guys," Donovan said, "to get rid of anything in the past. You gotta move on to the next play."

Living in the present is the best way to get to the future.

ROCKY TOPPED 2

By **KEVIN BROCKWAY**, *Sun sports writer*

Joakim Noah's blood spilled on the floor. Al Horford grabbed offensive rebound after offensive rebound. And Lee Humphrey sank a huge three-pointer that almost brought Florida all the way back.

But any last Florida hopes for the top spot of the SEC East came down to one possession and a mistake.

Dane Bradshaw's steal of an in-bounds pass from Corey Brewer and breakaway lay-up was the deciding bucket in a 76-72 Tennessee win over Gators that left a rocking O'Connell Center in stunned silence.

"You could say I lost the game for us again," Brewer said.

Brewer turned the ball over in the closing seconds of Florida's loss last month, leading to a deciding Bradshaw basket in a 80-76 loss at Tennessee. This one stung more. Tied at 72, Florida coach Billy Donovan called a timeout with 18.8 seconds left to set up a potential game-winning attempt.

But on the in-bounds play, Brewer didn't see Bradshaw as he attempted a soft bounce pass to teammate Al Horford. The first option was supposed to be point guard Taurean Green. The second option was supposed to be Humphrey.

"The guards were supposed to pop out and get the ball, but it didn't work out that way," Horford said. "We just didn't execute that well."

Brewer said he thought about calling a time out. "I probably should have," he said.

Tennessee coach Bruce Pearl said he set up for a steal on the in-bounds.

"We took a chance and we put Major Wingate in the game," Pearl said. "With 18 seconds left, on the road, I didn't want overtime. We put him on the ball because we hadn't stopped Florida late. So we said, let's make a play here. Who else but Dane Bradshaw could come up with the ball?"

OPPOSITE PAGE: Tennessee's C.J. Watson elbows Joakim Noah in the face after pulling in a rebound. Watson was called for an offensive foul. *Tracy Wilcox/The Gainesville Sun*

FEBRUARY 22, 2006

Lofton made both free throws, clinching the Tennessee sweep of the regular-season series. The Vols (20-4, 11-2 SEC East) clinched at least a tie for first in the division, with Florida (22-5, 8-5) dropping into a second-place tie with Kentucky.

Afterward, Donovan chalked up the loss to a young team experiencing growing pains.

"As a basketball team you have to go through it," Donovan said. "They need it. The game came down to our inexperience on the basketball court to their experience."

The loss was the fourth for Florida this season with the game tied in the final two minutes.

"You can say we're a young team, but that's just an excuse," Brewer said. "We have to learn to stop making mistakes in close games like this."

Lost in the meltdown were two clutch shots that tied the game late for UF. The first, a three-pointer by Brewer with 1:36 left, knotted the score at 69. The second, from Humphrey off an offensive rebound from Horford, tied it at 72 with 52.1 seconds remaining.

Noah led Florida with 20 points, with Brewer adding 17 and Chris Richard scoring all 14 of his points off the bench in the first half.

Turnovers proved to be Florida's undoing in the second half. The Gators committed 11 after intermission, including nine during a 12-minute stretch that netted just 12 Florida points.

"A lot of it was their slapping, their reaching, their grabbing, experienced ways they know how

Bradshaw drove in to put the Vols up 74-72, then Brewer attempted an open three-point attempt from the right side with 7.3 seconds remaining. It clanged off the front of the rim. Chris Lofton grabbed the rebound and was fouled by Humphrey before time expired.

to do things," Donovan said. "I don't want to say they frustrated us, but they made things difficult."

Lofton, who came into the game making 29 of his last 41 three-point attempts, led Tennessee with 16 points. Bradshaw added 15 and C.J. Watson scored 13 points.

Watson was involved in a chippy play with Noah late. He was called for an offensive foul after throwing an elbow in the face of Noah while trying to clear out an offensive rebound. Noah left the floor with blood running down his face.

After the game, Donovan said Noah lost a tooth as a result of the elbow.

"I don't know about him for the next game," Donovan said. "It's inside his lip. He's probably going to have to get it stitched up."

The Gators came into the game intent on stopping Lofton, throwing a variety of defensive looks at the 6-foot-2 sophomore guard. Brewer began guarding him man-to-man, with a double-team extended at the three-point line.

It worked early. Lofton was held to just one basket, a fall-away three-pointer, through the game's first 17 minutes.

On the offensive end, Florida pounded it inside. Richard made all seven of his first-half attempts. Up 26-23, Florida extended its largest lead of the game to 13 with a 10-0 run.

Lofton heated up late in the half, sparking a Tennessee run with a flurry of threes. Lofton sank threes on consecutive trips down the floor to pull the Vols within 36-31. After a Richard turnaround shot extended the Florida lead back to 38-31, Lofton struck again on a questionable play.

After Brewer missed a driving lay-up, Patterson appeared to have tripped him underneath the basket, allowing Lofton to break free on the right wing. Lofton sank the three to pull Tennessee within 38-34 with 1:04 left. Officials reviewed the tape after the play, but it was to check whether Lofton's foot was on the three-point line.

After Noah made two free throws with 33.8 seconds to put Florida back up 40-34, Wingate hit a bank shot with 9.8 seconds left. Florida had two chances to extend the lead, but Brewer couldn't convert on a driving lay-up, and Richard couldn't convert on an in-bounds play at the buzzer, sending Florida into the locker room up 40-36 at halftime.

	1st	2nd	Total
Tennessee	36	40	76
Florida	40	32	72

Tennessee

Player	FGM-A	3FGM-A	FTM-A	O-D REB	TP	A	BLK	S
Patterson	4-10	0-0	0-1	4-3	8	2	2	1
Wingate	5-6	0-0	1-1	0-0	11	0	1	0
Lofton	4-10	4-9	4-4	1-4	16	1	0	3
Bradshaw	6-13	3-6	0-1	2-2	15	5	0	4
Watson	6-11	1-1	0-0	0-6	13	3	0	0
Smith	3-6	3-5	0-0	0-0	9	3	0	0
Asumnu	2-4	0-0	0-0	0-2	4	0	0	1
Howell	0-0	0-0	0-0	0-1	0	0	0	0
Childress	0-0	0-0	0-0	0-0	0	1	0	0
Totals	30-60 (50.0%)	11-21 (52.4%)	5-7 (71.4%)	7-18	76	15	3	9

Florida

Player	FGM-A	3FGM-A	FTM-A	O-D REB	TP	A	BLK	S
Brewer	7-19	2-6	1-3	1-3	17	4	1	1
Noah	7-11	0-0	6-8	3-6	20	2	5	5
Horford	3-8	0-1	4-6	2-3	10	2	2	2
Green	2-8	0-2	0-0	0-2	4	3	0	1
Hodge	0-0	0-0	2-3	0-1	2	3	0	1
Moss	0-0	0-0	0-0	1-1	0	0	0	2
Humphrey	1-5	1-4	2-2	1-2	5	1	0	0
Richard	7-7	0-0	0-0	3-3	14	0	0	0
Huertas	0-0	0-0	0-0	1-1	0	0	0	0
Totals	27-58 (46.6%)	3-13 (23.1%)	15-22 (68.2%)	12-22	72	15	8	12

#12 LEE HUMPHREY

By Kevin Brockway, *Sun sports writer*

Through its third Final Four run in school history, the impact of Florida's four starting sophomores has hit the national landscape.

From the pony-tailed Joakim Noah swatting shots and scoring underneath, to the equally adept inside play of Al Horford, to the stifling defense of Corey Brewer, to the steady ball handling of point guard Taurean Green, the talent of the self-proclaimed "04s" has drawn comparisons to Michigan's Fab Five as among the best classes in college basketball history.

But what about the other guy?

In essence, Florida junior guard Lee Humphrey is like the fifth Beatle, a steady starter who would just as soon let the spotlight shine someplace else. Only teammates view Humphrey's role as vital. A 45.6-percent three-point shooter with a school-record 103 three-pointers, Humphrey has kept opposing defenses honest.

"If he weren't out there, it would be a lot harder," Noah said. "Even if he does not hit the shots, which he has been, it opens up the floor for the rest of us."

The bond between Humphrey and the sophomore class formed last year. As a sophomore, Humphrey teamed with the four, then freshman, in practice to scrimmage against the upperclassmen.

Humphrey and reserve forward Chris Richard are the only surviving members of the class of 2003. Point guard Ryan Appleby transferred after his freshman year and is now at Washington. Forward Mohamed Abukar transferred to San Diego State before his second semester as a sophomore.

With little left in his own class, Humphrey gravitated toward the younger guys.

"I don't know if I'm an adopted member or not," Humphrey said. "I definitely get along with those guys really well. C-Rich and I still like to claim the '03 class, I guess. I don't mind being called an adopted member."

Noah calls Humphrey "Humpty" and loves riding in the red jeep that Humphrey brought to campus last fall from his native Maryville, Tennessee.

There is a too-good-to-be-true side to Humphrey, who always answers questions with a smile and patience. He shuns bars for books.

"We play around with him, like Lee, we've got to take you out to the clubs, show you around," Horford said. "But he's not like that."

Humphrey said a typical Friday or Saturday night is spent watching movies at his friends' apartments. His favorite is Gladiator. For laughs, he'll watch Adam Sandler movies.

"There's been an occasional Friday where I'll study," Humphrey said. "But that's rare."

At the end of last season, following Florida's first SEC Tournament win in school history, Humphrey showed up to Matt Walsh's house for a party. It was one of Humphrey's few social outings with his teammates. He didn't stay long.

"He went there for an hour and just disappeared," Horford said.

The nightlife is not for Humphrey. Some who may have been skeptical about his bike accident last January didn't understand that Humphrey is not one you would find out late at night stumbling down a flight of stairs.

"That's not his thing, going out to clubs and stuff like that," Horford said. "He'd rather just stay at home and chill."

Humphrey earned SEC basketball scholar athlete of the year honors with a 3.71 GPA in applied kinesiology, the study of how muscles, nerves and organs relate to each other.

Some first-hand experience came when Humphrey took a spill on his bike, resulting in a separated left shoulder. Humphrey missed one game and lingered through dis-

Michael C. Weimar/The Gainesville Sun

Name: Lee Humphrey
Hometown: Maryville, TN
Attended: Maryville H.S.
Year: Junior
Major: Physical Education
Position: Guard
Height: 6-foot-2
Weight: 180 pounds

comfort for seven others before returning to the starting lineup February 26 against Alabama.

At that time, Florida coach Billy Donovan challenged Humphrey to shoot more. Humphrey responded by making 4 of 6, second-half, three-point attempts.

Since, Humphrey is 42.6 percent from three-point range, but the recovery of his shoulder re-established what Donovan believes is the most underrated aspect of his game.

"Lee might be one of the best shooters I've coached, but what he doesn't get enough credit for is his ability to defend on his perimeter," Donovan said. "He's probably our most consistent defender in terms of keeping guys in front of him and challenging shots."

It's fitting, in a way, that Humphrey is appearing in his first Final Four in Indianapolis. A huge Colts fan, Humphrey has an autographed Peyton Manning Tennessee Vols jersey framed in his room in Maryville.

"Pretty neat, huh," Humphrey said.

Neat enough to help carry Florida basketball to the brink of making history.

MARCH 1, 2006

NOAH SAVES UF

By KEVIN BROCKWAY, *Sun sports writer*

Even with a superhuman effort from 6-foot-11 forward Joakim Noah, Florida found itself in a familiar anxious situation against Georgia.

Few expected a tight game on Senior Night at the O'Connell Center against undermanned Georgia. But here it was, the Bulldogs down four, with the ball, two minutes remaining.

It was a chance for more heartache. But with a big rebound from Noah, a big three-pointer from Taurean Green and some sharp decision-making down the stretch, the 17th-ranked Gators (23-6, 9-6 SEC) outlasted Georgia 77-66 to snap their first three-game losing streak in close to three years.

Noah scored 37 points, the most for a Gator player at the O'Connell Center since Vernon Delancy's 38 against Alabama on January 24, 1981. Noah also set a school record for free throws made,

going 19-of-22 from the line. Neal Walk had the previous record with 18 in 1968.

"Whatever it takes to get a win," Noah said. "I'm happy. We needed to pull this one off."

Noah added 11 rebounds, the biggest coming with 1:55 remaining and Florida up 69-65. After a miss from Georgia center Dave Bliss inside, Noah put himself in position for the board and Mike Mercer fouled him from behind. Noah made 1-of-2 free throws.

After Georgia's Steve Newman missed a three-point attempt, Green sank a three-pointer at the other end with 52.5 seconds left to put Florida up 73-65.

OPPOSITE PAGE: Joakim Noah makes a strong move to the hoop against Georgia's Dave Bliss. Noah scored 37 points to lead the Gators to a win over the Bulldogs.
Tracy Wilcox/The Gainesville Sun

Green and sophomore forward Corey Brewer made four free throws down the stretch to seal it, even after Brewer was called for a questionable traveling call late.

"I still feel it's a learning and growing process for our guys," Florida coach Billy Donovan said. "I'm shocked, unbelievably surprised, that we're 23-6. We've obviously lost a lot of close games, but if you would have told me that Brewer would be out for a stretch and Lee Humphrey would have a separated shoulder, I would have told you we would have had some problems."

There were signs that Florida learned from its previous mistakes. With 2:22 left, Lee Humphrey called a timeout on an in-bounds play rather than forcing the ball. On the second in-bounds play, Green made the correct cut, and nearly scored on a breakaway lay-up.

"I guess you could say we're learning," Brewer said.

"Effort has never been a problem with these guys," Donovan said. "Our problem has been our guys not understanding and not recognizing certain situations."

Brewer added 13 points for Florida, and Green overcame a season-high seven turnovers with eight points and seven assists.

Florida needed a big night from Noah early because sophomore center Al Horford was limited to just 5 minutes in the first half with a hip pointer. Horford came back to play 17 minutes in the second half and came up with a big block late.

"He should be OK for Kentucky," Donovan said.

Freshman Mike Mercer led Georgia with 16 points, pulling the Bulldogs within 69-65 on a runner in the lane with 2:39 remaining. But the Bulldogs had no answer for Noah, who consistently beat Bliss and forward Younes Idrissi inside.

"We just tried to stand straight up, but he kept getting to the free throw line," Bliss said. "We just could not deny him the basketball."

Senior forward Adrian Moss, in his final O'Connell Center game, finished with two points and six rebounds in six minutes. Moss, who started in place of Noah, wasn't shy about putting it up. He attempted five shots, including a three-pointer, during a sluggish Florida first half. The Gators started with little energy, but still built a 13-point lead that was cut to 36-28 at halftime on a Mercer lay-up with 11 seconds remaining.

Moss' father, Cornelius, and brother Tremaine, were at center court during a pregame ceremony in which Moss was presented with his framed No. 4 jersey.

Noah played in front of his father, ex-French Open champion Yannick Noah, and for the first time in front of his grandfather, Zacharie, a former professional soccer player who came from Cameroon to watch his grandson play.

"I don't know if you can play harder because I think I always play hard," Noah said. "You feel like you're flowing when you are out there. When your family is out there, it's just extra inspiration."

Green had an idea that this roommate was going to have a big game.

"I was taking a nap in the afternoon and he was screaming and saying, 'It's game time, let's go,'" Green said. "It was hours before the game and he was still fired up."

Ironically, it was Noah off the bench who came up with the huge night.

"He carried our team offensively," Donovan said.

	1st	2nd	Total
Georgia	28	38	66
Florida	36	41	77

Georgia

Player	FGM-A	3FGM-A	FTM-A	O-D REB	TP	A	BLK	S
Idrissi	5-14	0-0	2-2	2-4	12	0	1	1
Bliss	2-5	0-0	2-3	3-4	6	0	1	0
Gaines	2-10	0-3	2-4	2-3	6	4	0	4
Stukes	1-6	1-6	0-0	0-2	3	2	0	1
Toney	4-4	0-0	0-0	0-0	8	3	0	1
Newman	1-4	0-2	0-0	0-0	2	1	0	0
Humphrey	4-9	2-5	1-1	2-2	11	0	0	2
Mercer	6-13	1-5	3-4	1-0	16	2	0	1
Singleton	1-1	0-0	0-2	0-0	2	1	1	0
Totals	26-66 (39.4%)	4-21 (19.0%)	10-16 (62.5%)	10-15	66	13	3	10

Florida

Player	FGM-A	3FGM-A	FTM-A	O-D REB	TP	A	BLK	S
Brewer	4-7	0-1	5-6	1-4	13	4	0	1
Moss	1-5	0-1	0-0	3-3	2	0	0	0
Horford	3-5	0-0	1-2	1-3	7	1	1	1
Green	2-5	2-3	2-2	0-3	8	7	1	0
Humphrey	3-7	2-5	0-0	0-2	8	1	0	1
Noah	9-14	0-0	19-22	2-9	37	1	1	0
Hodge	0-3	0-1	0-0	1-0	0	1	0	0
Richard	1-2	0-0	0-0	1-5	2	1	0	0
Huertas	0-0	0-0	0-0	0-0	0	0	0	0
Totals	23-48 (47.9%)	4-11 (36.4%)	27-32 (84.4%)	9-29	77	16	3	3

KENTUCKY FRIED

By KEVIN BROCKWAY, *Sun sports writer*

It was a surreal scene—seconds winding down; walk-ons in the game; cavernous Rupp Arena strangely silent. Kentucky's senior day was spoiled.

With some big second-half shots from Lee Humphrey and stout rebounding throughout, Florida beat Kentucky 79-64 for its first win at Rupp since 1998 and the most lopsided of its five wins in the building.

Florida (24-6, 10-6 SEC) secured the No. 2 East seed in the SEC Tournament in a game that was won on the glass. Florida outrebounded Kentucky 39-27, scoring 13 second-chance points and 36 points in the paint.

Humphrey led Florida with 17 points, with Joakim Noah adding 15 points and 11 rebounds and Al Horford scoring 13 points and grabbing nine rebounds.

Up 34-33 at halftime, Florida started the second half with an 11-2 spurt and maintained a lead near double-digits for the rest of the game.

"When we play with that hunger, we're a completely different team," Noah said. "For some reason, we're always on edge when we play Kentucky because we know they're a good team with a lot of tradition. We have to carry that over into every game we play."

Confidence-wise, Florida will take a two-game winning streak into the postseason after dropping its previous three.

"To win a game defending and rebounding, that's the biggest thing," Horford said. "That's what the coaches have been trying to stress to us. That's how you win games."

OPPOSITE PAGE: Lee Humphrey drives under pressure from Kentucky's Rajon Rondo. *Andy Lyons/Getty Images*

ABOVE: Alone in the lane, Chris Richard pulls down a rebound. Richard finished the game with six rebounds.
Andy Lyons/Getty Images

Florida extended its winning streak against Kentucky to four for the first time in school history. In SEC history, only Tennessee and Vanderbilt had beaten Kentucky four straight times.

"It doesn't matter," Noah said. "What does that mean? It won't mean anything if we don't go out and play well in March. People don't remember stuff like that. They remember teams that go to the Final Four."

Kentucky sophomore guard Joe Crawford led all scorers with 21 points. Sophomore center Randolph Morris added 14 points for the Wildcats (19-11, 9-7), who honored seniors Patrick Sparks, Ravi Moss, Brandon Stockton and Preston LeMaster in pregame ceremonies.

Kentucky fell to 81-5 all-time on senior day and a pedestrian 10-5 at home this season.

"It was a tough game and a tough way for our seniors to go out," Kentucky coach Tubby Smith said. "Overall we didn't play well."

Said Stockton: "They outworked us. They wanted it more than we did."

Much of the Big Blue noise that preceded the game—talk of Kentucky players having something for Noah for his chest-thumping celebrations—was silenced at the opening tip. Noah scored nine of Florida's first 24 points, with a bank shot in the lane giving the Gators an early 24-17 lead.

"It's easy to talk the talk," Noah said. "You've got to walk the walk, do it on the court."

But with Taurean Green and Corey Brewer in early foul trouble, Kentucky regrouped. Brewer was called for his second foul at the 12:12 mark.

Green was whistled for his second with 9:57 remaining.

Kentucky went on a 14-5 run, with a three-pointer from Ravi Moss giving the Wildcats a 31-29 lead with 3:47 remaining in the half. But Florida was able to stay close with freshmen Walter Hodge and David Huertas in the game. Hodge, who scored seven of his nine points in the first half, hit a baseline jumper to tie the score at 31.

"I was really concerned at that point, but David Huertas and Walter Hodge did such a great job," Florida coach Billy Donovan said. "I really didn't want to get our guys back out there and it worked out."

In the second half, Florida continued to pound the ball inside, with Noah, Horford and reserve Chris Richard (eight points, six rebounds), dominating the glass. Down 51-42, Kentucky had a chance to cut into the lead, but Rajon Rondo missed two straight free throws.

Humphrey (4-of-11 from three-point range) then sank threes on consecutive trips down the floor, the second putting Florida up 57-43 with 10:55 remaining.

"I just saw a kid letting it go and shooting it with a lot of confidence," Donovan said. "He was 4-of-11, but this could have been a game where he was 8-of-11 because he had such good looks and our big guys were doing such a good job kicking the ball back out to him. But for him to be aggressive like that, it's great to see."

Said Humphrey, who had his highest point total since returning from a separated shoulder in mid-February: "I felt pretty good out there. My shoulder feels like it's close to all the way back. I'm back weightlifting again. I feel stronger."

"It really doesn't mean anything other than playing one more game," Donovan said. "I know a lot was made of it but it wasn't like we were playing for an SEC Championship or something big at stake. It's nice, but we still have to go there and win games."

	1st	2nd	Total
Florida	34	45	79
Kentucky	33	31	64

Florida

Player	FGM-A	3FGM-A	FTM-A	O-D REB	TP	A	BLK	S
Brewer	3-5	1-1	0-0	0-1	7	5	0	0
Noah	6-8	0-0	3-4	5-6	15	3	4	0
Horford	4-10	0-0	5-7	4-5	13	4	1	0
Green	2-7	1-5	2-2	0-2	7	1	0	1
Humphrey	6-14	4-11	1-4	0-4	17	3	0	0
Swanson	0-0	0-0	0-0	0-0	0	0	0	0
Moss	0-1	0-0	0-0	0-0	0	0	0	0
Hodge	4-5	1-2	0-0	0-0	9	2	0	0
Berry	0-0	0-0	0-0	0-0	0	0	0	0
Tyler	0-0	0-0	0-0	0-0	0	0	0	0
Richard	4-5	0-0	0-0	3-3	8	0	0	0
Huertas	1-3	1-2	0-0	3-1	3	0	0	1
Totals	30-58 (51.7%)	8-21 (38.1%)	11-17 (64.7%)	13-22	79	18	5	2

Kentucky

Player	FGM-A	3FGM-A	FTM-A	O-D REB	TP	A	BLK	S
Obrzut	0-0	0-0	0-0	0-0	0	0	0	0
Stockton	2-5	1-1	2-2	0-0	7	2	0	1
Moss	3-7	2-5	0-0	0-2	8	2	0	0
LeMaster	0-2	0-2	0-0	0-0	0	0	0	0
Sparks	3-10	1-6	1-1	1-2	8	2	0	0
Rondo	2-6	0-1	0-2	1-1	4	4	0	3
Perry	1-7	0-2	0-0	3-3	2	0	1	1
Alleyne	0-0	0-0	0-0	0-0	0	0	0	0
Thomas	0-1	0-0	0-0	1-1	0	1	0	0
Williams	0-0	0-0	0-0	0-1	0	0	0	0
Crawford	6-10	2-6	7-9	0-3	21	0	0	0
Morris	5-9	0-0	4-7	2-3	14	0	1	1
Sims	0-1	0-1	0-0	0-0	0	0	0	0
Carter	0-0	0-0	0-0	0-0	0	0	0	0
Totals	22-58 (37.9%)	6-24 (25.0%)	14-21 (66.7%)	18-16	64	11	2	6

"When we play with that hunger, we're a completely different team."

—Joakim Noah
Florida forward

NEXT STOP: SEMIFINALS

By KEVIN BROCKWAY, *Sun sports writer*

With some offense from its guards, and a stellar home-state return for junior Lee Humphrey, Florida began the defense of its SEC Tournament title looking much like the team that won it in Atlanta a season ago.

Humphrey scored a career-high 25 points and point guard Taurean Green added 20, lifting Florida to a 74-71 win over Arkansas in the tournament quarterfinals.

"Coach has been on me to shoot with confidence," said Humphrey, who went 5-for-9 from three-point range. "It paid off tonight."

"When he's letting it go and shooting with confidence like that, it makes us a different team," Florida coach Billy Donovan said. "Some days, it might not be his night, but we need for him to continue to be aggressive."

There were a few dicey moments late, with Arkansas pulling within 72-69 on a three-pointer from Charles Thomas with 12.9 seconds remaining. But Humphrey sank two free throws with 9.4 seconds to seal the game.

"I've been shooting them pretty good in practice," said Humphrey, who came into the game 6-of-13 from the line but made all four attempts. "I'm glad they went down in the game."

Humphrey put on a shooting display in front of family and friends, who made the two-and-a-half hour drive from his hometown of Maryville, Tennessee.

For the game, Florida shot 10-of-15 from three-point range, its highest percentage of the season. Green was a perfect 5-for-5 from beyond the arc, with Humphrey at 5-of-9.

OPPOSITE PAGE: Lee Humphrey penetrates the Arkansas defense and lays up a shot in the lane. Humphrey led the Gators with 25 points. *Michael C. Weimar/The Gainesville Sun*

MARCH 10, 2006

Florida avenged an 85-81 overtime loss at Arkansas last month and snapped the Razorbacks' six-game winning streak.

Ronnie Brewer led Arkansas (21-9) with 18 points, with Thomas adding 17 and Jonathan Modica scoring 13.

A Ronnie Brewer three-pointer pulled Arkansas within a point, 37-36. But Florida responded with a 9-0 run. Horford, Corey Brewer and Noah scored consecutive baskets inside. Green capped it with a three-pointer from the top of the circle, putting Florida up 46-36 with 13:50 left.

Florida held the lead for the remainder of the game.

Florida received a scare when forward Corey Brewer hobbled off the court in the first half, favoring the same right ankle he sprained January 22 at Tennessee. But he returned at the 5:31 mark and played the rest of the game.

Offensively, Humphrey carried Florida early in the return to his native state. Humphrey scored Florida's first five points on a three-pointer and nifty spin move to the basket.

By the end of the half, Humphrey was two shy of his career high with 16 points, going 4-for-6 from three-point range.

Humphrey's fourth three-pointer of the half put Florida up 28-18, and a Noah put-back extended Florida's lead to 32-20 with 6:02 remaining. But the Gators managed just one point the rest of the half.

During the stretch, with Green on the bench, the Gators turned the ball over on six straight possessions.

Brewer and Vincent Hunter combined for nine straight Arkansas points during the stretch, with a Hunter lay-in pulling Arkansas within 32-29. Noah ended the scoreless drought with a free throw with 1:15 remaining, giving Florida a 33-29 lead it took into halftime.

Florida committed 17 turnovers but continued its strong play on the glass, outrebounding Arkansas 36-27.

	1st	2nd	Total
Arkansas	29	42	71
Florida	33	41	74

Arkansas

Player	FGM-A	3FGM-A	FTM-A	O-D REB	TP	A	BLK	S
Thomas	7-13	2-3	1-2	2-0	17	1	0	1
Hill	1-2	0-0	0-0	0-2	2	0	2	1
Brewer	6-11	2-3	4-4	1-6	18	4	0	6
Ferguson	2-13	1-7	1-1	0-1	6	2	0	1
Modica	4-8	1-3	4-4	1-0	13	1	0	0
Jefferson	0-0	0-0	0-0	0-0	0	1	0	0
Townes	2-6	0-0	1-2	2-3	5	1	1	1
McCurdy	1-4	0-3	0-0	1-1	2	4	0	0
Hunter	3-5	0-2	2-2	2-1	8	0	1	0
Totals	26-62	6-21	13-15	9-14	71	14	4	10
	(41.9%)	(28.6%)	(86.7%)					

Florida

Player	FGM-A	3FGM-A	FTM-A	O-D REB	TP	A	BLK	S
Brewer	4-9	0-1	1-2	2-2	9	1	0	1
Noah	2-9	0-0	5-6	3-3	9	0	1	0
Horford	4-7	0-0	3-6	1-7	11	0	2	0
Green	6-8	5-5	3-4	0-6	20	5	0	1
Humphrey	8-14	5-9	4-4	0-4	25	2	0	1
Moss	0-2	0-0	0-0	3-0	0	1	0	0
Hodge	0-0	0-0	0-0	0-1	0	0	0	0
Richard	0-0	0-0	0-0	0-1	0	1	0	0
Totals	24-49	10-15	16-22	9-24	74	10	3	3
	(49.0%)	(66.7%)	(72.7%)					

MARCH 11, 2006

RETURN ENGAGEMENT

By **KEVIN BROCKWAY,** *Sun sports writer*

Bring on the Gamecocks.

That was the message Florida players sent following their 81-65 semifinal win over LSU that set up an unlikely third meeting with South Carolina in the Southeastern Conference Tournament finals.

Florida advanced to its third straight title game and will try for its second straight tournament championship against a South Carolina team that posted two surprising wins against the Gators during the regular season.

"I hoped for this," sophomore Florida forward Corey Brewer said. "We wanted this. We had a bad taste in our mouth. We were able to get revenge against Arkansas. Now we want revenge against South Carolina, too."

Said sophomore forward Joakim Noah: "I'm very, very, very excited...I think that's something for us as Gators, I think that was definitely a game we wanted. Whether it was the championship or not, and to face them in the championship is definitely a dream for us."

South Carolina beat Florida 68-62 in Columbia in January, snapping a nine-game Florida winning streak in the series. The Gamecocks then came to Gainesville and won 71-67 in a game decided in the final two minutes.

"We gave them the first game," Brewer said. "We weren't mentally ready to play. The second game, it came down to the end. So we'll be ready now."

Florida (26-6) reached the finals by wearing down LSU late. Momentum shifted when Corey Brewer drew a charge from LSU center Glen Davis,

OPPOSITE PAGE: Joakim Noah reaches high above LSU's Glen "Big Baby" Davis for a rebound.
Michael C. Weimar/The Gainesville Sun

ABOVE: Corey Brewer watches as his lay-up finds the bottom of the net. *Michael C. Weimar/The Gainesville Sun*

drawing his fourth foul with 8:12 left. Florida, up 58-56 at the time, went on a 14-3 run, with point guard Taurean Green scoring the last eight on consecutive three-pointers and a driving lay-up that extended the Florida lead to 72-59 with 4:18 left.

Florida coach Billy Donovan wasn't happy with the defensive intensity in the first half and drew a technical while bartering for some early calls down low. But Florida responded at halftime, holding LSU to eight field goals in the second half.

"Taurean hit a couple of big shots for us, but I think it really came down to our ability to get some stops," Donovan said.

Green led Florida with 18 points. Noah added 15 points and 12 rebounds and Brewer chipped in with 15 points.

"I feel fresher," said Green, who scored 20 the night before against Arkansas. "I feel like I was at the beginning of the year. Coach has been doing a good job giving me some extra rest."

Davis, the SEC player of the year, was in foul trouble throughout. The 6-foot-9, 310-pound forward was held to 12 points after tying a career-high with 28 points the night before against Vanderbilt.

"Glen could never get in the rhythm he did for us last night," LSU coach John Brady said.

Point guard Darrel Mitchell led LSU with 21 points, with freshman Tasmin Mitchell adding 20.

LSU, the SEC regular-season champs at 14-2, played without freshman of the year forward Tyrus Thomas, who was out with a sprained ankle.

"Florida is quite good," Brady said. "They're well-coached. They're talented. Their team seems to fit together well and for us to beat them we had to be, you know, at full strength."

The win may have cemented an opening-round NCAA Tournament berth in the Jacksonville region, because Florida will likely climb to a top-four seed regardless of today's outcome. A win against South Carolina today would ensure that.

For now, though, the focus is on South Carolina. And on revenge.

"The past means nothing," senior forward Adrian Moss said. "It really doesn't matter until you get out there and play."

"Taurean hit a couple of big shots for us, but I think it really came down to our ability to get some stops."

—Billy Donovan
Florida head coach

	1st	2nd	Total
Florida	38	43	81
Louisiana State	41	24	65

Florida

Player	FGM-A	3FGM-A	FTM-A	O-D REB	TP	A	BLK	S
Brewer	6-9	1-3	2-2	0-0	15	0	0	1
Noah	7-11	0-0	1-4	6-6	15	4	0	1
Horford	4-5	0-0	2-2	0-2	10	1	2	0
Green	5-13	3-8	5-5	0-3	18	3	0	6
Humphrey	2-7	2-7	3-6	0-2	9	0	0	1
Swanson	0-0	0-0	0-0	0-0	0	0	0	0
Moss	2-4	0-0	0-0	1-0	4	0	1	0
Hodge	0-0	0-0	0-0	1-0	0	2	0	0
Berry	0-0	0-0	0-0	0-0	0	0	0	0
Tyler	0-0	0-0	0-0	0-0	0	0	0	0
Richard	5-8	0-0	0-1	2-5	10	1	0	0
Huertas	0-0	0-0	0-0	0-0	0	0	0	0
Totals	31-57 (54.4%)	6-18 (33.3%)	13-20 (65.0%)	10-18	81	11	3	9

LSU

Player	FGM-A	3FGM-A	FTM-A	O-D REB	TP	A	BLK	S
Davis	5-12	0-0	2-3	2-5	12	0	0	0
Mitchell	8-14	2-6	2-2	5-4	20	1	0	3
Lazare	4-6	0-0	2-4	0-1	10	0	0	1
Temple	1-6	0-4	0-0	0-2	2	2	0	0
Mitchell	6-14	3-9	6-7	1-2	21	6	0	0
Voogd	0-0	0-0	0-0	0-1	0	2	0	1
Rolle	0-2	0-0	0-2	2-2	0	0	2	1
Johnson	0-0	0-0	0-0	0-0	0	0	0	0
Totals	24-54 (44.4%)	5-19 (26.3%)	12-18 (66.7%)	10-17	65	11	2	6

TOURNEY TWO-PEAT

By KEVIN BROCKWAY, *Sun sports writer*

It was a scene few could have envisioned last October—hugs, Gator chomps and senior Adrian Moss draping the winning tournament jersey around his neck.

This was supposed to be a rebuilding season for Florida, with three new starters and two freshman guards coming off the bench.

Some picked the Gators fifth in the SEC East.

Yet Florida left March as conference tournament champions again, winning the SEC Tournament final, 49-47, in a furious finish.

Six-foot-11 sophomore forward Joakim Noah, one of the three new starters, scored the go-ahead basket, catching a Corey Brewer air ball and banking in a shot from the right side with 11.6 seconds remaining. Noah was there at the end, too, blocking a Renaldo Balkman shot in the closing seconds to secure the win.

Balkman, South Carolina's energizer all tournament, lay motionless on the court as the final buzzer sounded. Florida forward Al Horford threw the ball high into the Gaylord Entertainment Center rafters. South Carolina could have received an automatic bid to the NCAA Tournament with a win. Instead, Florida locked up a No. 3 seed in Jacksonville and will open the NCAA Tournament against South Alabama.

"We worked so hard this summer," said Brewer, who scored a team-high 16 points in the win. "It's about this right now. And tournament time, we want to make a run in the NCAA Tournament now."

OPPOSITE PAGE: Taurean Green clowns around during the celebration following Florida's SEC tournament championship win over South Carolina.
Michael C. Weimar/The Gainesville Sun

Asked how satisfying it was to repeat as tournament champions, Brewer responded: "It ain't satisfying yet. We're trying to make a run, make a point in the NCAA Tournament. After that, we'll tell you if it's satisfying or not."

Florida point guard Taurean Green earned tournament MVP honors. Green finished with 10 points and three assists, overcoming a season-high eight

ABOVE: Corey Brewer goes for the reverse lay-up over South Carolina's Tarence Kinsey. *Michael C. Weimar/The Gainesville Sun*
OPPOSITE PAGE: Taurean Green dishes the ball as he penetrates in the lane. *Michael C. Weimar/The Gainesville Sun*

turnovers. Balkman, Tarence Kinsey and Tre Kelley led the Gamecocks with 12 points apiece.

The final 11.6 seconds of drama made up for a game filled with ugly stretches. Florida kept the Gamecocks in the game by committing 18 turnovers and allowing 15 offensive rebounds. The Gamecocks simply couldn't shoot, finishing the game 30 percent from the floor and 22.2 percent from three-point range.

Florida was outrebounded for the first time in five games, albeit by a slim 32-31 margin. The 6-foot-8 Balkman was in position to tie the game when he caught a deflected shot from South

Carolina point guard Tre Kelley, who drove the length of the floor on the game's final possession. But Noah was in position to swat Balkman's shot attempt.

"He was a monster," Noah said of Balkman. "You just can't keep him off the glass. I think he underestimated my height a little bit. And thank God we got the block."

ABOVE: Head coach Billy Donovan cuts down the net after the Gators beat the Gamecocks for the SEC tournament championship. *Michael C. Weimar/The Gainesville Sun*

"You play it out and give your team a chance to win it and we did," Odom said. "All you want is a chance. We had that chance. I have no regrets."

Florida became just the third team to repeat as SEC tournament champs since its revival in 1979. Kentucky was the last to do it, winning back-to-back tournament titles in 2003 and 2004. Alabama is the only other school in the league to repeat, winning three straight titles from 1988-90.

"People only remember champions," Green said. "We're just trying to build a dynasty. Trying to turn this around into a basketball program."

Gone is the curse of Steve Spurrier, by a slim margin. Florida appeared in good position up 47-39 when Green fed Chris Richard for a lay-up inside with 4:42 left. But the Gators went cold after that, unable to score for the next 4:31. During the stretch, Green missed two open three-point attempts, including an air ball with 1:02 left.

South Carolina pulled within 47-45 when Rocky Trice sank two free throws with 1:29 left after being fouled inexplicably by Brewer at the three-point line. After the Green miss, Trice tied it with a runner in the lane with 43 seconds to go.

Florida coach Billy Donovan called a timeout with 21 seconds left, instructing Brewer to drive toward the basket and draw Noah's defender to him, in order for Noah to be in position to grab the rebound. Brewer did one better by floating an air ball that Noah caught and banked in.

Florida started in a 2-3 zone, daring South Carolina to shoot over it. The Gamecocks couldn't. South Carolina made just three of its first 21 shots and were unable to hit a jumper through the game's first 16 minutes.

Still, Florida couldn't pull away, leading just 25-18 at halftime due to nine first-half turnovers.

"Self-inflicted wounds," Donovan said. "All just self-inflicted. We contributed to them getting back in the game with our mental errors."

Fatigue also played a factor. South Carolina was playing its fourth game in four days, Florida its third in three days.

"Both teams were fatigued at the end, but that's something you got to play through," Green said.

Florida played through it for a surprising second straight tournament title. For Moss, who was the first to cut down the nets, it was an emotional way to end his SEC career.

"We've proved a lot of people wrong this year," Moss said. "We've got another ring to show for it."

	1st	2nd	Total
South Carolina	18	29	47
Florida	25	24	49

South Carolina

Player	FGM-A	3FGM-A	FTM-A	O-D REB	TP	A	BLK	S
Tisby	1-2	0-0	0-0	0-0	2	0	0	0
Kinsey	4-14	2-7	2-3	2-5	12	3	0	4
Wallace	1-3	0-2	0-0	2-1	2	2	1	1
Kelley	4-17	3-11	1-3	3-0	12	1	0	2
Trice	1-2	0-0	2-2	1-2	4	1	0	0
Sheldon	1-6	1-5	0-0	0-0	3	0	0	0
Palacios	0-1	0-0	0-0	0-0	0	1	0	1
Day	0-2	0-2	0-0	0-1	0	0	0	0
Balkman	6-13	0-0	0-0	6-5	12	1	1	4
Totals	18-60 (30.0%)	6-27 (22.2%)	5-8 (62.5%)	14-14	47	9	2	12

Florida

Player	FGM-A	3FGM-A	FTM-A	O-D REB	TP	A	BLK	S
Brewer	7-11	2-2	0-0	1-6	16	1	0	2
Noah	4-6	0-0	0-0	1-6	8	2	2	0
Horford	2-6	0-0	2-2	1-2	6	3	0	0
Green	4-11	2-6	0-0	0-2	10	3	0	1
Humphrey	1-3	1-2	0-0	0-3	3	2	0	0
Moss	0-0	0-0	0-0	0-3	0	0	0	0
Hodge	0-0	0-0	2-2	0-0	2	0	0	1
Richard	2-4	0-0	0-0	1-3	4	0	0	0
Totals	20-41 (48.8%)	5-10 (50.0%)	4-4 (100 %)	4-25	49	11	2	4

"*People only remember champions. We're just trying to build a dynasty. Trying to turn this around into a basketball program.*"

—Taurean Green

Florida guard

MARCH 16, 2006

GATORS GET MESSAGE

By KEVIN BROCKWAY, *Sun sports writer*

It started with ill-advised shots, poor ball movement and some barking between Florida coach Billy Donovan and point guard Taurean Green.

It ended with slam dunks on the break, swished three-pointers and pretty bounce passes in the lane.

Third-seeded Florida advanced to the second round of the NCAA Tournament with a 76-50 win over 14th-seed South Alabama that was anything but a rout through the first 20 minutes.

"Survive and advance," said sophomore forward Joakim Noah, whose all-around floor game sparked Florida in the second half. "That's what it's all about this time of year."

Lee Humphrey led four Florida players in double-figures with 20 points. The 6-foot-11 Noah added 16 points, 8 rebounds, 7 assists and 5 of Florida's 7 blocks.

Unable to establish inside scoring, Florida (28-6) muddled through some early stretches, leading 31-25 at halftime. Florida took a surprising 15 3-point attempts in the first half against a South Alabama team whose tallest starting post player was 6-foot-7.

"They were kind of baiting us into it a little bit," Donovan said. "I thought we took the bait at times."

But behind a partisan Florida crowd of 13,772 at Veterans Memorial Arena, the offense started to click in the final 20 minutes. Humphrey sparked Florida with the first of his four second-half three-pointers. Another Humphrey three put Florida ahead 44-33. Noah and Al Horford followed with consecutive inside baskets, with a Horford jump hook in the lane putting Florida ahead to stay 50-36.

Humphrey's six three-pointers set a Florida record for threes in an NCAA Tournament game,

OPPOSITE PAGE: After powering to the hoop, Al Horford throws down a dunk over his South Alabama defender.
Tracy Wilcox/The Gainesville Sun

surpassing the five that Anthony Roberson made against Sam Houston State as a freshman in 2003.

"We did a much better job moving the ball inside out in the second half," Donovan said. "Taurean didn't have a great shooting night, but I thought he had some good looks and did a good job the second half running our team."

Early, Florida was unable to get the ball inside to Noah and Horford. At the 9:52 mark in the first half, with Florida up 14-10, Donovan railed into Green. While the motive of the tirade was unclear, it woke Florida up through some early offensive doldrums.

"It was a little frustrating, but I think that our staying together was something helpful if we want to do something special," Noah said. "You learn from your experiences, and even though I was frustrated in the first half, we definitely did a better job driving into the paint in the second. That was something we spoke about in the locker room."

In an emotional game between Donovan and his former top assistant, South Alabama's John Pelphrey, neither team could find the bottom of the basket early. Combined, both teams missed their first 12 shot attempts before a Humphrey lay-up in the lane broke the lid on scoring at the 16:31 mark.

Florida led by as many as 11 in the first half, jumping to 31-20 with 2:04 remaining when a Horford steal in the lane set up a Noah breakaway dunk. But South Alabama (24-7) scored the last five points in the half, on a Mario Jointer lay-in and a Demetric Bennett three-pointer with 34.3 seconds left that pulled South Alabama within 31-20 at halftime.

Leandro Buboltz, who sank three first-half three-pointers to keep the Jaguars in the game early,

> *"Survive and advance. That's what it's all about this time of year."*
> —Joakim Noah
> Florida forward

led South Alabama with 14 points. Jointer added 10 points.

"Our goal was to take the inside away and keep them from jamming it down our throats because they have such good post players," Pelphrey said. "We did a good job of that in the first half. In the second half, it got away from us a little bit."

For the game, Florida held South Alabama to 34.5 percent shooting from the floor and forced 16 South Alabama turnovers. Florida also outrebounded the size-challenged Jaguars 39-31.

"In the first half, offensively, we were just OK," Donovan said. "We won because we played well defensively and we rebounded pretty well."

OPPOSITE PAGE: Joakim Noah puts the brakes on a drive by South Alabama's Richard Law. *Tracy Wilcox/The Gainesville Sun*

MARCH 18, 2006

NCAA TOURNAMENT, ROUND 2
JACKSONVILLE VETERANS MEMORIAL ARENA, JACKSONVILLE, FLORIDA

HOW SWEET IT IS

By KEVIN BROCKWAY, *Sun sports writer*

As the final seconds ticked away and the Gators' first trip to the Sweet 16 since 2000 became a certainty, Joakim Noah turned to teammates Taurean Green and Corey Brewer and pumped his fist onto his chest.

"We've got a long way to go, baby," Noah told them.

Third-seeded Florida (29-6) advanced past the second round of the NCAA Tournament for the first time in six years with a thorough 82-60 dismantling of 11th-seed Wisconsin-Milwaukee before 13,777 at Veterans Memorial Arena.

Florida's last trip to the Sweet 16 ended with a run to the NCAA Finals, where it lost to Michigan State.

This team has similar designs. Brewer acknowledged that he laughed earlier this week about the questions whether Florida would break its six-year Sweet 16 hex. In Brewer's mind, these Gators are capable of a run to the Final Four.

"I felt it all along," Brewer said. "When you play with guys the whole year and you know what they bring to your team, you just put all the ingredients together. You feel good about certain teams. You feel they are special. This is one team I feel like is very special."

Brewer led Florida with 23 points. Noah added 17 points, seven rebounds, six assists and four blocks. With Brewer and Al Horford (13 points, six rebounds) in early foul trouble, senior Adrian Moss provided a lift off the bench with six points and a season-high nine rebounds.

OPPOSITE PAGE: Corey Brewer fights through the UW defense and puts up a shot. Brewer led the Gators with 23 points. *Tracy Wilcox/The Gainesville Sun*

MARCH 18, 2006

Ahead 34-26 at halftime, Florida didn't play like a team nervous about another potential early exit. Instead, the Gators methodically pounded the ball inside. Florida outscored Wisconsin-Milwaukee in the paint 40-28, maintaining a double-digit lead for the final 10 minutes of the second half.

"We had good balance," Florida coach Billy Donovan said. "Our frontcourt players did a good job in and around the basket. Corey did a good job shooting the basketball."

There was no fear of failure. "We don't worry about stuff like that," Noah said.

Defensively, Florida maintained its edge. The Gators held Wisconsin-Milwaukee to 36.1 percent shooting, effectively containing leading scorers Boo Davis and Joah Tucker. Davis, who scored 26 in Wisconsin-Milwaukee's opening-round upset of Oklahoma, was held to 10 points on 3-of-12 shooting. Tucker had nine points. Senior 6-foot-7 center Adrian Tigert led the Panthers (22-9) with 27 points.

"I was concerned about trying to double him," Donovan said. "I wanted him to score and to take those other guys out of the game the best we could. It worked out for us."

Said Davis: "They made me work hard on both ends and I didn't have a lot of good looks. The confidence wasn't really there. It was just a difficult night for me."

Wisconsin-Milwaukee cut Florida's lead to 34-29 on a Tigert three-pointer to start the second half. But Brewer responded with the first of his three, second-half three-pointers. A Brewer jumper in the lane put Florida up 41-31. Noah followed with a pretty spin move in the lane past Tigert for a dunk, extending Florida's lead to 43-31 and erupting the partisan Florida crowd into a frenzy.

Florida executed its plan to exploit its size advantage inside early. Horford scored Florida's first basket on a dunk on a feed from Noah. Brewer left the game with Florida up 14-9 after drawing his second foul on a charge. Brewer hit his head hard on the court on the play.

"I was a little woozy," Brewer said. "But they did a good job getting some

fluids in me and I felt fine in the second half."

Brewer's 23 were three shy of the career-high 26 he scored last month against Vanderbilt.

"Corey was feeling it," Noah said. "That was huge for us."

Florida led by as many as 13 points in the first half when a Horford jump hook in the lane put the Gators ahead 24-11. But Wisconsin-Milwaukee responded with a 9-0 run, pulling to within 24-20 on two Tigert free throws.

Walter Hodge and Moss followed with consecutive baskets inside to put Florida back up 28-20. Noah scored Florida's last two baskets of the half on a dunk and a jumper, and Florida forced a Davis miss on Wisconsin-Milwaukee's final possession to go into halftime ahead 34-26.

"Our goal here is to win it," Noah said. "If there was anyone on our team who is saying, 'OK, we're good now,' I'd be disappointed.

"We wake up at 6 a.m. in the offseason throwing up, guys in tears because they are in so much pain. That's what we go through. There are times when we're running and everyone is sleeping in their beds. We're out there just sweating for this. That's the test right now. We've got to be ready."

ABOVE: Greeting Gator fans after the game, Corey Brewer celebrates his team's win over UW-Milwaukee in the second round of the NCAA tournament.
Tracy Wilcox/The Gainesville Sun
OPPOSITE PAGE: Leading the fast break, Joakim Noah races up-court past Panthers guard Avery Smith (3).
Tracy Wilcox/The Gainesville Sun

	1st	2nd	Total
Wisconsin-Milwaukee	26	34	60
Florida	34	48	82

Wisconsin-Milwaukee

Player	FGM-A	3FGM-A	FTM-A	O-D REB	TP	A	BLK	S
Tucker	4-14	1-5	0-0	0-2	9	2	0	0
McCoy	2-3	0-1	0-1	0-1	4	1	1	1
Tigert	11-13	2-2	3-4	2-6	27	3	1	0
Hill	0-6	0-4	0-1	2-2	0	2	1	1
Davis	3-12	2-4	2-3	4-5	10	2	0	3
Massiah	0-0	0-0	0-0	0-0	0	0	0	0
Smith	0-3	0-0	2-4	1-2	2	0	0	1
Pancratz	0-2	0-0	2-2	1-0	2	0	0	0
Hanson	2-3	2-3	0-0	1-0	6	0	0	0
Hansen	0-0	0-0	0-0	0-0	0	0	0	0
Bendall	0-0	0-0	0-2	0-0	0	0	0	0
Young	0-2	0-1	0-0	1-0	0	0	0	0
Ford	0-3	0-0	0-0	2-0	0	0	0	0
Totals	22-61 (36.1%)	7-20 (35.0%)	9-17 (52.9%)	14-18	60	10	3	6

Florida

Player	FGM-A	3FGM-A	FTM-A	O-D REB	TP	A	BLK	S
Brewer	9-16	5-8	0-0	2-1	23	0	1	1
Noah	5-10	0-0	7-9	1-6	17	6	4	2
Horford	6-8	0-0	1-3	2-4	13	2	0	0
Green	2-6	1-4	2-2	0-2	7	6	1	0
Humphrey	3-7	2-6	1-1	1-1	9	2	0	2
Swanson	0-0	0-0	0-0	0-0	0	0	0	0
Moss	3-5	0-1	0-0	3-6	6	0	0	1
Hodge	1-2	0-1	0-0	0-3	2	1	0	0
Berry	0-0	0-0	0-0	0-0	0	0	0	0
Tyler	0-0	0-0	0-0	0-0	0	0	0	0
Richard	1-2	0-0	3-4	0-4	5	0	1	0
Huertas	0-0	0-0	0-0	0-0	0	0	0	0
Totals	30-56 (53.6%)	8-20 (40.0%)	14-19 (73.7%)	11-27	82	17	7	6

BILLY DONOVAN

By Pat Dooley, *Sun sports writer*

This is the perception of the tournament, that the last dancers have the best choreographers.

Billy Donovan is suddenly a brilliant strategist because Corey Brewer threw in a shot against Georgetown. The more teams can't make three-pointers, the smarter Donovan becomes. Get good match-ups and you've figured out how to win in March.

Donovan has always made it clear that he will not fall into the trap of defining his teams based on their tournament performances. The same goes for his coaching ability.

"Am I a better coach this year than I was last year?" he asked after Florida advanced to the Sweet 16 in Jacksonville. "Probably not."

But to those who follow the Gators only when the regular season is over, Donovan has made a major jump in the coaching ranks simply by winning four games, three against teams seeded seventh or lower.

The truth is that Donovan will get too much credit for this run just as he received too much blame when the Gators were getting knocked out on the first weekend.

All of this is simply perspective to be added to the following statement—Billy Donovan is a lot better coach than he was in 2000 when the Gators made their last Final Four appearance.

And he should be. He was 34 then, only a half-dozen years into his head coaching career. Today, he is 40, wisdom stacked from a decade in the conference and eight years in the postseason.

He has a better idea about how to make a run like this and a better idea how there is a lot more than coaching that goes into it. Really, it's about players and match-ups. And sometimes luck.

But there is no question that the maturation process has taken place.

"I hope as a coach, the experiences you go through, you get better, you improve," Donovan said.

He says the difference between Billy 2000 and Billy 2006 is that he appreciates how much everyone else enjoys a ride like this one.

"I get so much more pleasure seeing other people be happy," Donovan said. "I'm not saying I was selfish before but I probably didn't take the time to see how much people enjoyed it."

There's much more than putting aside self-absorption to the new Donovan. The changes are subtle and can only be observed if you've actually seen the Gators play games over the last seven years.

He has changed, but some of it is real and some perceived.

There is a perception, for example, that Donovan finally figured out that you can't win with a bunch of McDonald's All-Americans because it puts too many egos on one team. So he went out and got guys who would stick around for four years and be great team players.

This would be true except for three things:

1. His 2000 team was loaded with McDonald's guys and went all the way to the national title game.

2. He has not stopped recruiting the best players in the country but has missed out on a handful in the last couple of years.

3. He could lose as many as three players to the NBA following this season.

Other than that...

The reality is that Donovan has changed his recruiting philosophy somewhat, but not as drastically as some people believe.

"Billy still wants talent as much as anybody, but I think he wants to make sure he gets the right McDonald's All-Americans," said assistant coach Donnie Jones.

Donovan was burned by a group of talented players who probably weren't right for Florida basketball—Christian Drejer, Ryan Appleby, Mohamed Abukar, etc. This group of Super Sophs was not a highly recruited bunch, but it's not like they were ignored.

Michael C. Weimar/The Gainesville Sun

Name: Billy Donovan
Season at UF: 10th
College: Providence (1983-87)
Position: Head Coach
Family: Wife, Christine, and four children:
William, Hasbrouck, Bryan, and Connor

It is with those players that we have seen one of the real improvements in Donovan's coaching. There was a knock on the Florida coach that players didn't show a lot of improvement after they entered the program. There were players who didn't get a lot better, but others like Udonis Haslem and Matt Bonner who showed drastic improvement.

This group should end that criticism for a long time.

Of course, in the end there are two ways to look at it. Donovan is in the Final Four so he must be improving as a head coach. Or Donovan has improved as a head coach so his team has made it to the Final Four.

Both are probably right.

FINAL FOUR IS GOAL

By KEVIN BROCKWAY, *Sun sports writer*

Courtesy of a remarkable shot from Corey Brewer, Florida is moving on to the Elite Eight.

Brewer's short jumper between two defenders with 27.5 seconds to go was the deciding bucket in a 57-53 win over Georgetown before 22,293 in the Metrodome.

To advance, Florida survived a game that was tight throughout, with neither team building a lead more than nine points. The Gators did it on a heads-up play from Brewer, who tracked down an offensive rebound in the lane after consecutive misses from Joakim Noah and Al Horford. Brewer drove to his right and was fouled by Georgetown forward Brandon Bowman as he rattled home an eight-foot jumper.

"I want to thank Corey Brewer for saving my butt after I missed a wide-open lay-up," Noah said.

Seventh-seeded Georgetown (23-10) went for the win on its final possession, but a three-pointer from reserve Bowman hit off the back iron with 7.5 seconds remaining. Horford was fouled by Georgetown center Roy Hibbert on the rebound, then made two free throws with 6.6 seconds left to seal it.

Florida won with scoring balance. Joakim Noah led UF scorers with 15 points. Taurean Green added 13 points with Horford scoring 12 points as the third Gator in double figures.

Jeff Green led Georgetown with 15 points, with point guard Ashanti Cook adding 12 points. The 7-foot-2 Hibbert finished with 10 points and seven rebounds.

OPPOSITE PAGE: Corey Brewer takes an off-balance shot in front of Georgetown's Darrel Owens (20).
Doug Finger/The Gainesville Sun

FLORIDA 57 | GEORGETOWN 53

Brewer atoned for an earlier error when he had an in-bounds play stolen in the final three minutes. Bowman made Florida pay with an open lay-in to put Georgetown ahead 51-49 with 2:37 left.

Lee Humphrey answered, putting Florida ahead 52-51 with a three-pointer from the right corner with 2:22 left. But Cook responded with a jumper in the lane that banked off the backboard, giving Georgetown a 53-52 lead with 1:55 left.

It was that way throughout, back and forth in a game that featured seven second-half lead changes.

Down 30-28 at halftime, Florida scored the first eight points of the second half. Green began the run with a three-pointer from the top of the circle. Noah and Horford followed with consecutive baskets inside, with Horford sinking 1-of-2 free throws to put Florida ahead 36-30.

Georgetown pulled within 36-34 on a Jonathan Wallace three-pointer, before Noah began asserting himself inside. A hook from Noah put Florida back up 38-34. After a Bowman lay-in, Noah was at it again, scoring on a put-back off a Walter Hodge miss and drawing Hibbert's third foul.

Noah's free throw put Florida up 41-36, but the lead was short-lived. Georgetown responded with an 8-1 run, regaining the lead on a wide-open dunk. But Noah answered with a dunk of his own on a pretty baseline drive, tying the score at 44.

From there, both teams traded baskets down the stretch. A Green three-pointer put Florida ahead 49-46, but Owens answered with a big three-pointer for Georgetown, knotting the score at 49 with 3:22 to go.

In its first Sweet 16 appearance since 2000, Florida played to Georgetown's plodding pace early. Florida's first two offensive possessions ended in a missed shot and turnover before Noah scored on a dunk in transition to tie the game at 2.

Hibbert made an early impact, scoring on a lay-up, setting up another basket with an offensive rebound and drawing a charge for Horford's first foul. With Hibbert on the bench, Georgetown turned to Cook and Green for offense. The two combined to score 22 of Georgetown's 30 first-half points.

A Green three-pointer pulled Florida within 12-10, but Georgetown responded with an 11-2 run sparked by Cook. Cook sank a three-pointer in the right corner and Hibbert followed with a dunk to give Georgetown a 17-10 lead. Noah followed with a dunk for Florida, but was called for a technical. Cook sank both free throws. Cook then scored on a driving lay-up to give Georgetown its biggest lead of the half, 21-12.

Florida pulled back close with defense, holding Georgetown scoreless during a 2:26 stretch. Brewer scored four straight points on a lay-up and two free throws. A Horford dunk pulled Florida within 21-20. Florida took its first lead of the game, 24-23, on a Horford tip-in with 5:45 remaining.

But Green answered with a three-pointer to put Georgetown back up 26-24. Horford then picked up

OPPOSITE PAGE: Georgetown forward Jeff Green can only watch as Al Horford throws down a slam dunk.
Doug Finger/The Gainesville Sun

MARCH 24, 2006

his second foul on a reach in and was forced to sit the final 5:11.

Florida rallied to take a 28-26 lead on a Brewer steal and breakaway dunk and a Chris Richard turnaround hook in the lane. But the Gators were

FLORIDA 57 | GEORGETOWN 53

held scoreless for the final 4:02 of the half, with Green missing shots on four straight possessions.

Georgetown regained the lead on Hibbert hook in the lane with 29.2 seconds left. Florida called timeout, but a Brewer turnaround jumper in the lane was short as time expired, leaving Florida trailing 30-28 at halftime.

Georgetown scored eight of its first-half baskets in the paint, with the other three coming from beyond three-point range.

	1st	2nd	Total
Georgetown	30	23	53
Florida	28	29	57

Georgetown

Player	FGM-A	3FGM-A	FTM-A	O-D REB	TP	A	BLK	S
Bowman	5-15	0-4	0-1	3-4	10	1	1	0
Green	5-10	1-1	4-5	3-3	15	4	0	2
Hibbert	5-9	0-0	0-0	2-5	10	0	3	0
Cook	4-8	2-5	2-2	0-0	12	3	0	2
Wallace	1-5	1-4	0-0	1-3	3	2	0	2
Owens	1-6	1-6	0-0	1-1	3	4	0	2
Sapp	0-1	0-1	0-0	2-3	0	1	0	0
Totals	21-54	5-21	6-8	12-19	53	15	4	8
	(38.9%)	(23.8%)	(75.0%)					

Florida

Player	FGM-A	3FGM-A	FTM-A	O-D REB	TP	A	BLK	S
Brewer	3-6	0-1	3-3	1-1	9	4	1	1
Noah	6-13	0-0	3-4	4-6	15	0	5	0
Horford	4-8	0-0	4-6	2-4	12	0	2	1
Green	3-9	3-7	4-4	0-3	13	2	0	0
Humphrey	2-7	2-5	0-0	0-4	6	1	0	0
Moss	0-0	0-0	0-0	1-0	0	0	0	0
Hodge	0-1	0-0	0-0	0-1	0	0	0	2
Richard	1-1	0-0	0-0	0-0	2	0	0	0
Totals	19-45	5-13	14-17	8-19	57	12	8	4
	(42.2%)	(38.5%)	(82.4%)					

MARCH 26, 2006

BACK TO INDY

By KEVIN BROCKWAY, *Sun sports writer*

In the hours leading up to its Elite Eight game against Villanova, Florida coach Billy Donovan didn't invite any motivational speakers or show any inspirational movies.

On the green chalkboard in the locker room, Donovan merely inscribed four capital letters in white chalk: T-E-A-M.

Florida advanced to its third Final Four in school history, taking the Minneapolis Region with a 75-62 win over Villanova that required contributions from everyone, even little-used freshman guard David Huertas.

Like in its last Final Four appearance in 2000, Florida will play in the RCA Dome in Indianapolis.

"It's every kid's dream, to go to the Final Four," said sophomore forward Corey Brewer, who battled through foul trouble throughout to finish with 11 points. "That's what you play college basketball for. But we have a chance to do something special now. We have a chance to win the first national championship in school history."

Florida has never won a national title in basketball, losing in the NCAA Finals in 2000 to Michigan State and losing in the national semifinals in 1994 to Duke.

"It's a great feeling now, but our goal is to win two more," said sophomore forward Joakim Noah, who earned region MVP honors following his 21-point, 15-rebound performance. "We're happy, but we can't be satisfied."

The celebration spilled from the floor, where Florida players danced in their Final Four hats, to the locker room, where Noah sang the Spice Girls

OPPOSITE PAGE: Coach Billy Donovan raises the net during the postgame celebration following UF's defeat of Villanova in the Elite Eight round of the NCAA tournament.
Doug Finger/The Gainesville Sun

song "2 become 1" as he was carted off for postgame interviews.

Florida moved on to its second Final Four under Donovan, who guided Florida to the 2000 NCAA finals.

"It's a totally different team," Donovan said. "This one is special because these kids have shown a level of selflessness and play the way the game should be played. They look out for each other. They care for each other. That shows on the court."

Many projected these Gators would have a lot of growing pains with the loss of Anthony Roberson, Matt Walsh and David Lee. Few predicted 20 wins, let alone 31-6.

"We had a lot of doubters in the beginning," Brewer said. "We've proved a lot of people wrong."

ABOVE: Lee Humphrey finger-rolls a lay-up after penetrating the lane. *Doug Finger/The Gainesville Sun*
OPPOSITE PAGE: Joakim Noah makes a powerful move to the basket under heavy pressure from Villanova freshman Dante Cunningham. Noah led the Gators in scoring with 21 points. *Doug Finger/The Gainesville Sun*

Said Noah: "At the end of the day, it made us a tighter unit."

In the process, Florida avenged a second-round NCAA Tournament loss to Villanova a season ago. This one was different from the outset. Florida established an inside presence early with Noah and sophomore forward Al Horford and managed to contain Villanova's quick four-guard lineup.

Horford added 12 points and 15 rebounds and point guard Taurean Green had 19 points and four assists.

Senior Randy Foye led Villanova with 25 points, with Allan Ray adding 11. The top-seed Wildcats were dreadful from the field, shooting 24.7 percent from the floor and 17.4 percent from three-point range.

Florida did much to alter shots inside, with the 6-foot-11 Noah and the 6-foot-9 Horford protecting the basket. Noah finished with five blocks, with Horford adding two. Florida outrebounded Villanova 53-40 despite giving up 26 offensive rebounds.

"We wanted to take away the three-point shot from Foye and Ray and make them settle for tough twos," Florida guard Lee Humphrey said.

Said Villanova coach Jay Wright, "Joakim was long enough that he could change shots without fouling."

The game plan worked, but not without some anxious moments. Noah and Horford combined to score Florida's first 13 points, and the Gators jumped ahead 25-16 on the Humphrey three-pointer. Florida extended the lead to 35-23 on two Green free throws, but with Green and Brewer in foul trouble, the Gators were held scoreless for the final

3:31, turning the ball over three times in its last six possessions. Villanova closed the half on a 7-0 run, with all its points coming from the free-throw line.

"I was a little concerned with our foul trouble and our turnovers late," Donovan said. "In the second half we did a much better job of taking care of the basketball."

Brewer was forced to sit the final 12:21 of the first half. Walter Hodge also picked up three first-half fouls, which made Donovan turn to a surprise contributor in Huertas. Huertas, who played just two minutes in two NCAA Tournament games and did not play Friday against Georgetown, finished with two points and three rebounds in 14 minutes.

Brewer returned to score the first four points of the second half, putting Florida ahead 39-30 on a jumper and driving lay-up to the basket.

Villanova cut the Florida lead to 45-42 on a Foye jumper with 11:15 left. From there, Florida returned to its game plan of getting the ball inside. Noah got to the line four times, sinking 7-of-8 free throws during the game-altering 17-8 run that put Florida up 62-50.

Foye pulled Villanova within 62-54 on a lay-in, but Horford and Noah teamed to finish the Wildcats off. Horford backed Villanova center Will Sheridan down in the lane, then found a cutting Noah underneath the basket for a wide open dunk.

In the postgame frenzy, Noah made his way to the Florida stands, where he hugged his mom, former Miss Sweden Cecilia Rodhe, and talked to his dad, ex-French Open champion Yannick Noah, on his cell phone. Former NBA center Tito Horford hugged his son, Al, who wore one of the regional nets around his neck.

For players, the joy was still sinking in.

"We just have to stay together and play basketball the way we know how to play," Noah said. "If we do that, we're capable of great things."

	1st	2nd	Total
Florida	35	40	75
Villanova	30	32	62

Florida

Player	FGM-A	3FGM-A	FTM-A	O-D REB	TP	A	BLK	S
Brewer	4-7	1-2	2-3	0-3	11	2	0	0
Noah	4-8	0-0	13-15	0-15	21	1	5	1
Horford	6-12	0-0	0-0	8-7	12	1	2	0
Green	3-9	1-4	12-13	1-1	19	4	0	1
Humphrey	3-12	2-9	0-0	1-1	8	4	0	0
Moss	0-0	0-0	0-0	1-1	0	0	0	0
Hodge	0-2	0-1	0-0	1-2	0	0	0	0
Richard	1-2	0-0	0-0	3-1	2	1	1	0
Huertas	1-2	0-1	0-0	2-1	2	1	0	0
Totals	22-54	4-17	27-31	17-32	75	14	8	2
	(40.7%)	(23.5%)	(87.1%)					

Villanova

Player	FGM-A	3FGM-A	FTM-A	O-D REB	TP	A	BLK	S
Foye	7-18	2-8	9-10	3-5	25	0	0	2
Ray	5-19	1-7	0-0	2-0	11	1	0	0
Sheridan	0-6	0-0	1-2	3-2	1	0	1	0
Lowry	1-9	0-0	1-1	2-2	3	2	1	2
Nardi	2-11	1-7	3-4	1-3	8	4	0	1
Benn	0-0	0-0	0-0	0-0	0	0	0	0
Fraser	1-4	0-0	7-7	5-2	9	1	4	0
Charles	0-0	0-0	0-0	0-0	0	0	0	0
Dunleavy	0-0	0-0	0-0	0-0	0	0	0	0
Anderson	0-2	0-1	1-2	1-0	1	0	0	0
Cunningham	1-2	0-0	0-1	1-0	2	0	0	1
Clark	1-2	0-0	0-0	4-0	2	0	0	0
Totals	18-73	4-23	22-27	22-14	62	8	6	6
	(24.7%)	(17.4%)	(81.5%)					

FLORIDA 75 | VILLANOVA 62

ABOVE: The Florida coaches embrace on the sideline after the final buzzer sounded and the Gators advanced to the Final Four.
Doug Finger/The Gainesville Sun

RIGHT: Al Horford (left) and Joakim Noah hitch a ride back to the locker room after eliminating Villanova from the NCAA tournament. *Doug Finger/The Gainesville Sun*

#2 COREY BREWER

By Pat Dooley, *Sun sports writer*

Corey Brewer's father never won the French Open like Joakim Noah's.

His father never scored 1,000 points in an NBA season like Taurean Green's.

His father was never a first-round NBA Draft pick like Al Horford's.

"He's a peon compared to those guys," Glenda Brewer said of her husband. "But Corey, he loves his daddy. They are tight."

The famous fathers of three of the four Super Sophs on this Florida basketball team have been visible and often quoted. Ellis Brewer, 60, has simply watched from the house in rural Portland, Tennessee, where he and Glenda raised tobacco, soybeans and a 6-foot-8 forward heading to the Final Four.

"I ain't done nothing," he said, "but grow up on a farm."

Ellis Brewer may not carry the high profile of the famous fathers, but he has had just as much impact on his high-flying son.

It's just that he had to go about it differently.

Noah, Horford and Green were inspired by celebrity status, leathered by travel and fueled by athletic genes. Brewer found his motivation in the tobacco fields.

"I tried to tell him he can't grow up like I did," Ellis said of his son. "I told him he had to get a good education. You have to know how to use a computer these days. You don't want to raise tobacco for a living."

Ellis Brewer no longer raises tobacco. He has had three operations—one open heart and two balloon catheters to open clogged veins—making it impossible to work the fields. Now, he owns a business that removes trash, one handed down by his late brother.

Besides, the message has already been delivered.

"He'd send me to the field by myself every summer since I was 5 years old, strip the tobacco, take away the trash," Brewer said. "Man, I took away some nasty trash. It makes you appreciate basketball a lot.

"I think it helped me toughen up. And he made it clear to me that I needed to go to college. Working in the field, man, that was a great lesson."

Brewer didn't just work in the field, he drove the tractor…at the age of 8. Never complained about anything, his mother said. Worked in the hot sun, then went and played basketball all afternoon.

He obviously was driven.

You motivate with what you have.

If you are adored by your countrymen or 15,000 in the Garden, it rubs off on your kid. He wants to follow in daddy's footsteps. If you've experienced the long days of manual labor, you want the footsteps to be avoided.

And the best way to do that is to let him walk in them for a while.

He's still trying.

Last summer, Brewer returned to the house in Portland where he grew up.

"My dad tried to make me go out in the field," Brewer said. "I said, 'Naw, dad, not no more.'"

Brewer's journey to Gainesville is so polar opposite of Noah or Horford, both born in foreign countries, but certainly in line with other success stories in college sports.

"It's a different path and different experiences," Noah said. "But we all have the same goals. I tell you, Corey Brewer is the man in Portland, Tennessee. When they have a parade there, he's sitting with the mayor."

The different paths have led them all to this point, two wins away from the first national title in the school's basketball history. Ellis and Glenda hope to be there. He doesn't want any part of an airplane, but the four-hour drive is tempting.

He has seen his son play once, at Vanderbilt this year, when he felt up to making a 32-mile trip.

"As soon as we came out of the locker room," said Horford, "we were all like, 'There's Mr. Brewer.' And we'd

Name: Corey Brewer
Hometown: Portland, TN
Attended: Portland H.S.
Year: Sophomore
Major: Social and Behavioral Science
Position: Forward
Height: 6-foot-8
Weight: 185 pounds

Doug Finger/The Gainesville Sun

never met him before. He looks just like him. Same smile and everything."

Glenda said father and son have the same skinny legs "except Corey can jump."

Some day, maybe soon, he'll jump all the way to the NBA. There is no tobacco farming in Corey Brewer's future because it was a part of his past.

His dad never became a pop star.

His dad never was a prized recruit.

His dad was never a head coach in college.

"My daddy's not famous," Brewer said. "But he's worked hard all his life."

Which makes him famous enough.

CINDERELLA IS DONE

By KEVIN BROCKWAY, *Sun sports writer*

Behind the outside shooting of Lee Humphrey and a dominant effort on the offensive glass, Florida moved a step closer to its first basketball national championship in school history.

Florida ended George Mason's storybook run, nearly leading throughout in a 73-58 win in a game that served notice that the Gators (32-6) weren't just happy to be here.

"All good stories have to come to an end," point guard Taurean Green said. "George Mason is a good team but we came here with a mission to win a national championship."

Added sophomore forward Corey Brewer: "The glass slipper is broken. Cinderella is done."

For the second time in six years, Florida is in the national title game, where it will face UCLA, which demolished LSU 59-45 in the other semifinal. In 2000, Florida made the national finals, also in Indianapolis, losing 89-76 to Michigan State. "It's a great feeling to be here, but if you don't get a win Monday night, it hurts just as much," sophomore forward Joakim Noah said. "The dream isn't over until we win a national championship."

Florida takes a 10-game winning streak and a feeling of destiny into the title game after knocking off the national underdog. The Gators are 19-0 against non-SEC teams this season.

George Mason (27-8) had beaten Michigan State, North Carolina and Connecticut to get to the Final Four, but couldn't contain Florida on the offensive boards. Florida outrebounded the 11th-seed Patriots 40-27, grabbing 10 of its 16 offensive rebounds in the first half.

OPPOSITE PAGE: Corey Brewer celebrates at the final buzzer as the Gators eliminated George Mason from the NCAA tournament in the semifinals, 73-58.
Michael C. Weimar/The Gainesville Sun

FLORIDA 73 | GEORGE MASON 58

In a fitting sequence to end the game, Florida grabbed three straight offensive rebounds, holding the ball for more than two minutes before punctuating the game with a Brewer three-pointer. The size advantage of 6-foot-11 Noah and 6-foot-9 center Al Horford was too much for George Mason's starting post tandem of Jai Lewis and Will Thomas, both 6-foot-7.

"Florida's ability to get so many second shots really hurt us," George Mason coach Jim Larranaga said. "It took away opportunities."

Humphrey and Brewer led Florida in scoring with 19 points apiece as a sellout at the RCA Dome watched four Florida players reach double figures.

Green added 15 points. Noah contributed with 12 points, eight rebounds and Horford had six points and 13 rebounds.

Lewis and Tony Skinn scored 13 apiece for the Patriots, who were held to 41.1 percent from the field.

Humphrey sank five of his six three-pointers in the second half. Humphrey's threes tied a career-high and tied for third most in RCA Dome history.

"I felt good the whole night shooting the ball," Humphrey said. "Coach always does a great job of telling me to keep shooting and instilling confidence in me."

"Florida's ability to get so many second shots really hurt us. It took away opportunities."

—Jim Larranaga
George Mason head coach

OPPOSITE PAGE: Guarding Taurean Green, George Mason's Tony Skinn tries to fight through Joakim Noah's screen.
Michael C. Weimar/The Gainesville Sun
RIGHT: Corey Brewer throws down an uncontested dunk on a fast break in the second half. Brewer scored 19 points in the UF win over George Mason.
Michael C. Weimar/The Gainesville Sun

"We were able to work it inside out," Florida coach Billy Donovan said. "Lee Humphrey shot it well. Taurean did a good job running our team. We had a little better balance in the second half and we still continued to defend the three."

Up 31-26 at halftime, Humphrey delivered the knockout, sinking three consecutive three-pointers to start the second half. The third, falling away from the basket with Skinn draped on him, put Florida ahead to stay at 40-28.

"Humpty was feeling it tonight," Noah said.

"Those threes were big," Green said. "It just opened the whole game up for us."

Overall, Florida went 12-of-25 from the three-point line, compared to 2-of-11 for George Mason.

"It's a matter of pick your poison," Florida senior forward Adrian Moss said. "They sagged down on our big guys and left our shooters open. They picked the wrong poison tonight."

A three-pointer from Folarin Campbell pulled George Mason within 64-55 with 5:05 left, but Green and Brewer responded with four straight free throws to build the lead back to 13.

Early in the game, Noah set the tone inside, blocking a Lewis lay-up attempt on the first possession of the contest. Florida threatened to end Mason's storybook run quickly, jumping ahead 16-6 on a Brewer three-pointer from the top of the circle with 10:22 remaining. But Noah, who struggled to finish inside in the first seven minutes, picked up his first foul at the 12:31 mark and headed for the

ABOVE: Al Horford dives over George Mason's Jai Lewis for a rebound. Horford led UF in rebounding with 13. *Michael C. Weimar/The Gainesville Sun*

OPPOSITE PAGE: George Mason's Chris Fleming covers his face as he walks off the court after Florida ended the Patriots' surprising tournament run. *Michael C. Weimar/The Gainesville Sun*

bench. With Noah out, George Mason responded with a 7-0 run. Skinn scored on a driving lay-up, and Lewis on a bank shot over Moss to cut the Florida lead to 16-13 with 10:22 left.

A Campbell jumper pulled George Mason within 18-17 with 7:18 left, but Florida responded with a 7-2 spurt.

Green, who came into the game shooting 31.6 from three-point range for the tournament, made 3-of-4 first-half attempts. Two big ones came late. After George Mason pulled to within 25-24 on a three-point play from Skinn, Green responded with a three-pointer from the top of the circle to put Florida up 28-24 with 2:01 remaining.

After a Campbell lay-up it was Green again hitting a three-pointer with 34.8 seconds remaining on a play kept alive on a tap-back from Horford. It was that way throughout the first half. Florida dominated the offensive glass, scoring 16 second-chance points off 10 offensive rebounds.

Green and Brewer combined to score 21 of Florida's 31 first-half points.

"We weren't happy with the way we were running our offense," Green said. "We knew we had to spread the ball out more and get the ball inside."

Florida played the role of national spoiler to perfection. Brewer acknowledged he was tired of watching George Mason on TV. Junior forward Chris Richard questioned whether George Mason had respect for Florida. "They had a great run," Horford said. "I'm happy for them. Now it's time to go win a championship."

	1st	2nd	Total
George Mason	26	32	58
Florida	31	42	73

George Mason

Player	FGM-A	3FGM-A	FTM-A	O-D REB	TP	A	BLK	S
Thomas	4-12	0-0	2-5	1-2	10	0	1	3
Lewis	5-13	0-1	3-3	6-5	13	1	0	2
Skinn	5-12	1-4	2-3	1-2	13	1	0	1
Butler	4-7	0-2	0-0	0-4	8	1	1	0
Campbell	3-5	1-2	3-3	0-1	10	0	0	0
Carter	0-0	0-0	0-0	0-0	0	0	0	0
Konate	0-0	0-0	0-0	0-0	0	0	0	0
Norwood	1-4	0-2	0-0	0-1	2	3	0	2
Burns	0-0	0-0	0-0	0-0	0	0	0	0
Fleming	0-0	0-0	0-0	0-0	0	0	0	0
Hernandez	1-3	0-0	0-0	2-0	2	0	0	0
Totals	23-56	2-11	10-14	10-15	58	6	2	8
	(41.1%)	(18.2%)	(71.4%)					

Florida

Player	FGM-A	3FGM-A	FTM-A	O-D REB	TP	A	BLK	S
Brewer	6-11	3-6	4-5	2-4	19	1	0	1
Noah	5-11	0-1	2-2	1-7	12	2	4	1
Horford	2-7	0-0	2-3	6-7	6	4	0	2
Green	3-9	3-6	6-6	2-1	15	0	0	2
Humphrey	6-12	6-12	1-3	0-3	19	0	0	1
Moss	0-1	0-0	0-0	0-0	0	0	0	0
Hodge	0-1	0-0	0-0	0-0	0	0	0	0
Richard	1-1	0-0	0-0	2-1	2	1	0	0
Huertas	0-0	0-0	0-0	0-0	0	0	0	0
Totals	23-53	12-25	15-19	13-23	73	8	4	5
	(43.4%)	(48.0%)	(78.9%)					

Tricia Coyne/The Gainesville Sun

APRIL 3, 2006

NCAA TOURNAMENT CHAMPIONSHIP
RCA DOME, INDIANAPOLIS, INDIANA

NATIONAL CHAMPIONS

By KEVIN BROCKWAY, *Sun sports writer*

Inside the locker room, moments after the mission was accomplished, strands of confetti spread across the blue carpet.

Sophomore forward Al Horford wore a strand of the winning basket above his ear. Senior forward Adrian Moss tied his to his national championship cap.

Florida won its first national championship in school history Monday night, beating UCLA 73-57 with the same poise and precision it had displayed through most of its 33-6 season. A season that began with a 17-game winning streak and ended with a streak of 11 straight wins came down to a game in which Florida displayed its selflessness and ability to defend.

"People were talking all Sunday about UCLA's defense, UCLA's defense," sophomore forward Corey Brewer said. "No one talked about our defense. We kind of took that personally."

Florida held UCLA to 36.1 percent from the field, 17.6 percent from three-point range. The Gators blocked 10 shots and had seven steals.

"I told them before the game, what do we want to be," Florida coach Billy Donovan said. "We wanted to do the things that we did to get to this point."

Offensively, it was one of Florida's most flawless efforts. The Gators dished 21 assists to six turnovers. Joakim Noah, the game's MVP, led four Florida players in double figures with 16 points. Lee Humphrey added 15 points. Horford had 14 points and Brewer scored 11 points with three steals.

OPPOSITE PAGE: MVP Joakim Noah holds a piece of the net and points to his father during the postgame celebration.
Michael C. Weimar/The Gainesville Sun

APRIL 3, 2006

"It says a lot about the kind of team we have," Horford said. "We worked together, like we have all season long."

Noah was the intimidator inside, blocking six shots to raise his total to an NCAA Tournament record 29 in six games.

"This feeling makes all the hard work, all the sweat, all the tears, all the sacrifice worthwhile," Noah said. "Everything about this feels good. It not only feels good. It smells good. It tastes good."

When UCLA tried to press late to get back into the game, Florida had an answer every time, scoring seven of its last nine baskets on dunks and lay-ups.

"They pressured us," said point guard Taurean Green, who had two points and 8 assists. "We knew if we could move the ball around and keep our composure, we could beat the pressure and get easy baskets."

The Gators were a team that looked out for each other all season long, even through a three-game skid at the end of February. The closeness was personified by the fact that sophomore starters Noah, Green, Horford and Brewer have lived together since their freshman year. Before the final seconds ticked away, Horford, Brewer and Noah held each other in a long embrace.

"It was a special moment," Brewer said. "We've lived together all year long, worked hard together all year long. We're like brothers."

The first national championship in the history of a Division I basketball team in the state of Florida will be rewarded with a rally today at Gainesville Raceway, a Thursday trip to the White House and a Friday celebration at the O'Connell Center. Florida's run through the NCAA tournament featured five wins in double figures, with the lone scare coming in a 57-53 Sweet 16 win against Georgetown.

ABOVE: Al Horford dunks easily on a fast break in front of Jordan Farmar in the second half. Horford scored 14 points against the Bruins, more than a few of them coming on dunks.
Michael C. Weimar/The Gainesville Sun
OPPOSITE PAGE: Corey Brewer reaches for a rebound above Jordan Farmar (1) and Luc Richard Mbah a Moute (23). Brewer pulled down seven rebounds for the Gators.
Michael C. Weimar/The Gainesville Sun

received a warm embrace from his former coach and mentor moments after the game. Donovan worked as a graduate assistant under Pitino at Kentucky from 1989-94. The year Donovan arrived at Florida, Pitino won his first national championship at Kentucky.

Pitino wore a blue and orange tie he bought when he found out Florida was heading for the Final Four.

"You always hope, for humble people who work hard, for something like this to happen," Pitino said. "It's a fairy tale, really."

Mentor and pupil were near tears.

"At first he didn't want to come on the floor," Donovan said. "He said it was my moment. But I told him, you are a part of this in getting me where I am today, just like our coaching staff, our players, our support personnel, everyone. Then I told him that I loved him."

"Coach, don't get mad, but we're going to do this up pretty big," Noah said.

Donovan, 40, joins select company in being the first coach other than Dean Smith and Bobby Knight to play in a Final Four and win a national championship. A Rick Pitino disciple, Donovan

For Florida, the season was a magical ride, one that began with the Gators unranked for the first time since 1998. Brewer sensed the season could be special when Florida won the Coaches vs. Cancer

APRIL 3, 2006

Tournament in November. Horford felt like a national championship was possible after Florida got out of the first weekend of the NCAA tournament for the first time since 2000, beating South Alabama and Wisconsin-Milwaukee in Jacksonville.

Fifth-year senior Adrian Moss, who provided a huge lift with nine points and five rebounds off the bench in his final game, sensed it even earlier.

"Even back in October, when everyone was doubting us," Moss said. "We knew we had what it took to be champions."

Already, there are thoughts of repeating, if sophomores Noah, Horford and Brewer decide to return for their junior seasons. There is speculation that all three could leave for the NBA Draft as projected first-rounders.

"The NBA can't do this," Noah said. "The NBA doesn't match this. We're champions."

Pressed further, Noah said: "We're going to enjoy this, and worry about that the next couple of weeks."

OPPOSITE PAGE: Uncontested, Joakim Noah dunks in the second half. Noah led Florida in scoring with 16 points.
Michael C. Weimar/The Gainesville Sun
BELOW: Al Horford blocks a UCLA shot as Lee Humphrey hits the deck. The Gators blocked 10 shots on the night, six of them by Joakim Noah—an NCAA tournament record.
Michael C. Weimar/The Gainesville Sun

If the team and coaching staff remain intact, it would be hard not to consider Florida the preseason No. 1. Asked about repeating, Donovan glanced down at his watch.

"How long has it been, about one hour," Donovan said. "No, you take a look at the programs like the Connecticuts, like the North Carolinas, like the Dukes, they have coaches that have been there, like 20 years. I've only had 10. But it's something I can tell you that we will keep working for and striving for."

Horford didn't count it out.

"I would love it," Horford said. "Bring all the boys back and try to do it again. That would be pretty special."

	1st	2nd	Total
Florida	36	37	73
UCLA	25	32	57

Florida

Player	FGM-A	3FGM-A	FTM-A	O-D REB	TP	A	BLK	S
Brewer	4-12	2-3	1-3	3-4	11	4	1	3
Noah	7-9	0-0	2-2	2-7	16	3	6	1
Horford	5-8	0-0	4-5	2-5	14	3	2	0
Green	1-9	0-7	0-1	0-4	2	8	0	1
Humphrey	4-8	4-8	3-3	0-1	15	2	0	0
Moss	3-6	0-0	3-4	2-4	9	0	0	0
Hodge	0-3	0-1	0-0	0-1	0	1	0	2
Richard	2-3	0-0	2-2	0-0	6	0	1	0
Totals	26-58 (44.8%)	6-19 (31.6%)	15-20 (75.0%)	9-26	73	21	10	7

UCLA

Player	FGM-A	3FGM-A	FTM-A	O-D REB	TP	A	BLK	S
Bozeman	2-3	0-0	5-6	0-3	9	3	0	0
Mbah a Moute	3-9	0-2	0-0	3-7	6	1	0	0
Hollins	4-10	0-0	2-2	5-5	10	0	1	0
Farmar	8-21	1-8	1-2	0-2	18	4	0	2
Afflalo	3-10	2-7	2-2	0-2	10	1	0	1
Collison	0-3	0-0	0-0	1-2	0	1	0	0
Aboya	1-1	0-0	0-2	2-1	2	0	0	0
Mata	1-4	0-0	0-0	2-3	2	0	0	0
Roll	0-0	0-0	0-0	0-0	0	0	0	0
Totals	22-61 (36.1%)	3-17 (17.6%)	10-14 (71.4%)	13-25	57	11	1	3

GREATEST GATORS EVER

By PAT DOOLEY, *Sun sports writer*

It was now Tuesday morning, after 1 a.m., and Billy Donovan was still saying it wasn't about him.

He was half-right.

It wasn't just about him. But it was about him.

It was about taking the job Rick Pitino said was a mistake, then embracing his mentor after winning a national title in year 10.

"I'll see Rick later," said Florida athletic director Jeremy Foley, "and I'm going to have a lot of fun with him."

It was about Foley, too, who took a chance on Donovan and gave him all the tools to produce this incredible night.

It was about all of the coaches who came before Donovan.

"Lon Kruger, Norm Sloan, they have a piece of this," Donovan said.

It was about the players who didn't win titles, guys who bought into Donovan's dream and were criticized for making early exits in the tournament. They kept giving Florida a chance and some of them sold Florida to the players who made up this championship team during recruiting visits.

It was about the assistant coaches who contributed so much to this team. They kept coming to the Big Dance and figuring out how to survive and advance.

Perfect example—during UCLA's semifinal win over LSU, Donnie Jones noticed that a Bruin assistant would hold up cards to call out plays like "Nevada" or "14-X." Every time they did it against Florida, Jones was yelling to his defenders what to expect.

OPPOSITE PAGE: After sinking a jump shot and getting fouled in the process, Corey Brewer gets a hug from Joakim Noah. Brewer scored 11 points and swiped three steals.
Michael C. Weimar/The Gainesville Sun

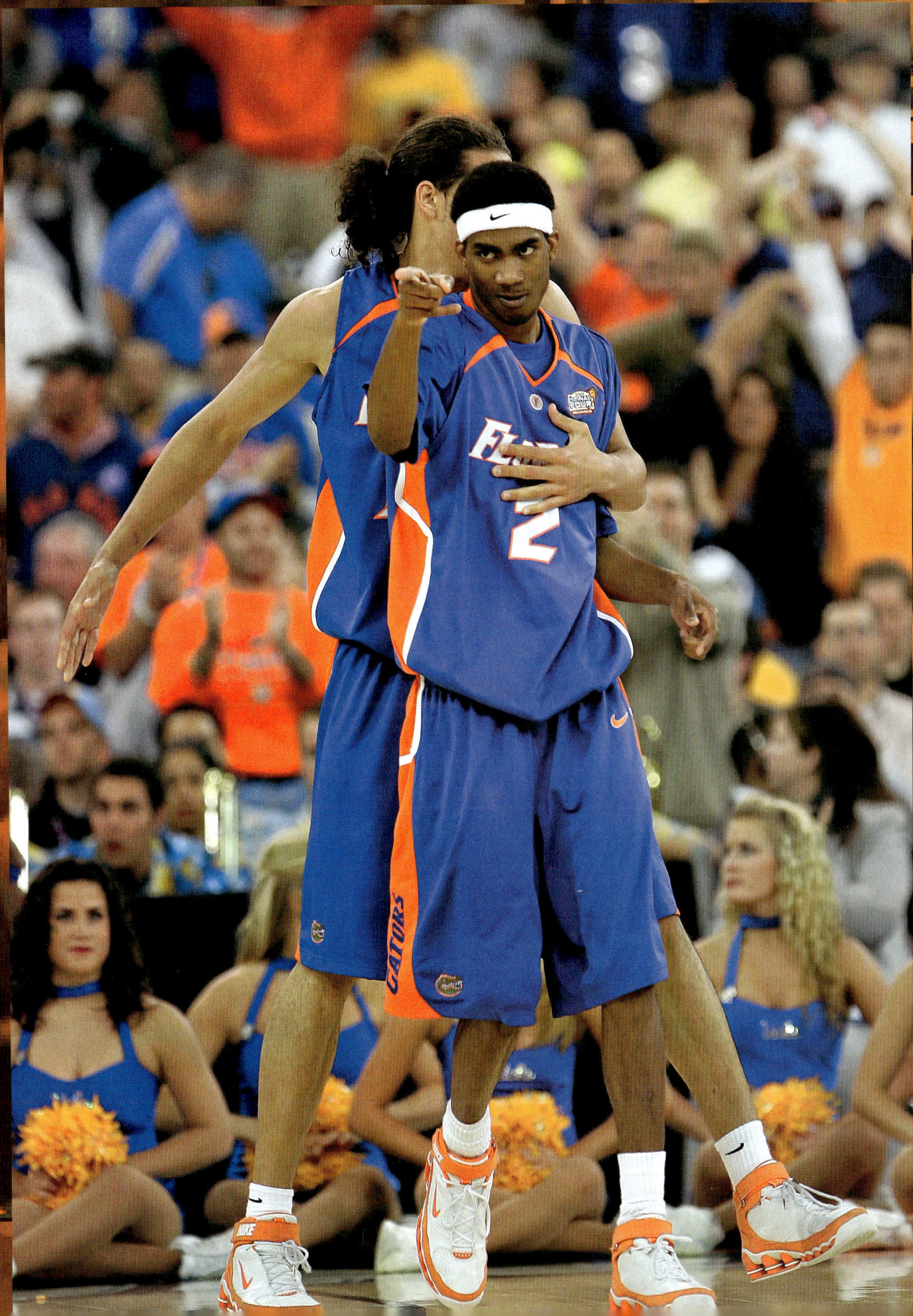
GATORS
2

And you saw the defense Florida played to easily handle UCLA.

It was about the players. They did it.

Whether they all come back or one or two or three leave didn't matter as they soaked in the adulation and the amazing feeling. "It's always a part of your thinking," Corey Brewer said. "If it feels this good, think how good it would feel to do it again."

It's about the fans who rocked the O-Dome and the thousands who made the trip to the RCA Dome. They sensed it could happen this year. They were rewarded.

Really, it's about everybody who has anything to do with Florida basketball, trainers and managers and secretaries.

Mostly, whether he wants to believe it or not, it was about Donovan.

"Nick Cassisi, our faculty adviser, said to me before the game that there's no better feeling than to build something from the ground level and build it all the way up," Donovan said.

And that's where Florida was when he arrived on campus. Ground Zero. Now, the Gators enjoy the confetti-filled rarified air of a champion.

They are among college basketball's elite.

"The Florida basketball program has taken it up a notch," Foley said. "I'm sure a lot of people considered 2000 (when Florida first played for a national title) a fluke. Now, we've done it. Will we do it again? Only time will tell.

"I never imagined what it would feel like because I didn't want to jinx it. It's almost surreal."

Donovan told his team before the game to go out and earn it.

"You're not playing for a national championship," he said. "You're playing for today. You have to not want this night to end."

On Sunday, as he walked into the arena for practice, Donovan said he noticed a list of the teams who have made the most Final Four appearances.

"Of course, it was Duke, and Kentucky and UCLA," he said. "You get in enough, you have a better chance of winning it. Sometimes I wish people would look at what Florida has done making it as much as we have.

"It's so hard to win. Someone wrote whether Corey Brewer's shot (against Georgetown) had the same impact as Mike Miller's (in 2000 against Butler). We were down one. If that doesn't go in maybe everybody's saying you had a good year, you made the Sweet 16. There's going to be peaks and valleys."

This is a peak like no other.

This is the greatest accomplishment of any Gator athletic team ever. Sure, the 1996 football title still resonates throughout the Gator Nation. But that team played for the championship the previous year. That team, and I'm not taking anything away from it, needed some breaks in other games.

This team that wasn't even supposed to be in the tournament at the beginning of the season rolled through it with incredible ease. One close game against Georgetown, the rest won by double-digit margins.

The Super Sophs, the Oh-fours, coming up big again. The bench playing one of its best games of the postseason, Adrian Moss saving his best game for his last.

The MVP of the tournament—Joakim Noah—closing out the greatest jump from one season to the next.

"I never let the media define who I was going to be," he said after the game.

We can define them all now.

The greatest Gators ever.

UCLA 57 TEAM 0   0 TOL 1 PLR-FL   FLORIDA 73

Andy Lyons/Getty Images

SEASON STATS

Player	GP	MIN	FG%	3FG%	FT%	REB	A	TO	BLK	S	TP
Noah	39	24.9	.627	.000	.733	7.1	80	76	95	43	552
Green	39	33.4	.366	.384	.886	2.9	184	124	5	50	519
Brewer	39	28.1	.468	.350	.769	4.8	128	108	16	58	494
Horford	39	25.9	.608	.000	.611	7.6	77	74	68	40	442
Humphrey	38	29.9	.475	.459	.600	1.9	72	39	0	28	415
Richard	39	17.5	.698	.000	.704	3.6	19	36	14	14	232
Hodge	39	19.2	.387	.368	.667	1.1	47	49	1	37	150
Moss	39	11.2	.465	.182	.667	2.4	18	26	5	11	122
Huertas	35	9.2	.378	.333	.765	1.5	23	15	1	6	87
Tyler	16	2.5	.417	.250	.857	0.6	0	3	2	2	17
Swanson	16	2.9	.364	.222	1.000	0.3	2	4	0	1	14
Berry	15	2.1	.375	.250	.500	0.4	0	1	0	0	8
Totals	39	—	.500	.392	.744	33.0	650	555	207	290	3052
Opponents	39	—	.399	.318	.666	32.1	432	605	107	284	2478

SEASON RESULTS

Date	Opponent	Location	Result	Leading Scorer
11/1/2005	Embry Riddle (Exh)	Gainesville, FL	W, 86-48	Noah, 21
11/4/2005	West Florida (Exh)	Gainesville, FL	W, 84-41	Green/Humphrey, 14
11/9/2005	St. Peter's College	Gainesville, FL	W, 80-51	Brewer, 18
11/10/2005	Albany	Gainesville, FL	W, 83-64	Brewer, 18
11/17/2005	Wake Forest	New York, NY	W, 77-72	Green, 23
11/18/2005	Syracuse	New York, NY	W, 75-70	Green, 23
11/25/2005	Florida State	Gainesville, FL	W, 74-66	Green, 15
11/28/2005	Alabama State	Gainesville, FL	W, 87-60	Green, 18
12/3/2005	UCF	Gainesville, FL	W, 80-47	Brewer, 25
12/6/2005	Providence	Providence, RI	W, 87-77	Green, 18
12/9/2005	Bethune Cookman	Gainesville, FL	W, 88-58	Horford, 17
12/18/2005	Jacksonville University	Gainesville, FL	W, 101-58	Noah, 21
12/22/2005	University of Miami	Miami, FL	W, 77-67	Noah, 18
12/30/2005	Florida A&M	Gainesville, FL	W, 84-47	Noah, 18
1/3/2006	Morgan State	Gainesville, FL	W, 92-49	Humphrey, 14
1/7/2006	Georgia	Athens, GA	W, 90-72	Noah, 24
1/11/2006	Mississippi State	Gainesville, FL	W, 75-60	Green, 20
1/14/2006	Auburn	Gainesville, FL	W, 69-57	Green, 21
1/18/2006	Savannah State	Gainesville, FL	W, 113-62	Noah, 21
1/21/2006	Tennessee	Knoxville, TN	L, 76-80	Brewer, 20
1/25/2006	South Carolina	Columbia, SC	L, 62-68	Green, 17
1/28/2006	Vanderbilt	Gainesville, FL	W, 81-58	Horford, 16
1/31/2006	Ole Miss	Oxford, MS	W, 69-58	Green, 17
2/4/2006	Kentucky	Gainesville, FL	W, 95-80	Green, 29
2/8/2006	South Carolina	Gainesville, FL	L, 67-71	Noah, 15
2/11/2006	LSU	Gainesville, FL	W, 71-62	Horford/Noah, 16
2/15/2006	Vanderbilt	Nashville, TN	W, 73-68	Brewer, 26
2/18/2006	Arkansas	Fayetteville, AR	L, 81-85	Green, 20
2/22/2006	Tennessee	Gainesville, FL	L, 72-76	Noah, 20
2/26/2006	Alabama	Tuscaloosa, AL	L, 77-82	Green, 20
3/1/2006	Georgia	Gainesville, FL	W, 77-66	Noah, 37
3/5/2006	Kentucky	Lexington, KY	W, 79-64	Humphrey, 17
3/10/2006	Arkansas	Nashville, TN	W, 74-71	Humphrey, 25
3/11/2006	LSU	Nashville, TN	W, 81-65	Green, 18
3/12/2006	South Carolina	Nashville, TN	W, 49-47	Brewer, 16
3/16/2006	South Alabama	Jacksonville, FL	W, 76-50	Humphrey, 20
3/18/2006	UW-Milwaukee	Jacksonville, FL	W, 82-60	Brewer, 23
3/24/2006	Georgetown	Minneapolis, MN	W, 57-53	Noah, 15
3/26/2006	Villanova	Minneapolis, MN	W, 75-62	Noah, 21
4/1/2006	George Mason	Indianapolis, IN	W, 73-58	Brewer,Humphrey, 19
4/3/2006	UCLA	Indianapolis, IN	W, 73-57	Noah, 16

Tricia Coyne/The Gainesville Sun

ACKNOWLEDGMENTS

The entire staff of *The Gainesville Sun* contributed to the coverage of the 2005-06 University of Florida men's basketball national championship season. The photography, design, graphics and sports department did the great bulk of the work.

PHOTOGRAPHY DEPARTMENT

Director of photography: Brian W. Kratzer
Assistant director of photography: Rob C. Witzel
Photographers: Michael C. Weimar, Doug Finger, Tracy Wilcox, Briana Brough, Jarrett Baker, Aaron Daye
Photo lab assistant: Morgan Petroski

DESIGN EDITOR

Rob Mack

SPORTS DEPARTMENT

Sports editor: Arnold Feliciano
Assistant sports editor: Jeff Barlis
Lead sports designer: Missi Koenigsberg
Columnists: Pat Dooley and Hubert Mizell
Reporters: Kevin Brockway, Robbie Andreu, Brandon Zimmerman, John Patton
Copy editor: Andres Buenaventura
Sports assistants: Jon McDonald, Talal Elmasry, Daniel Shanks

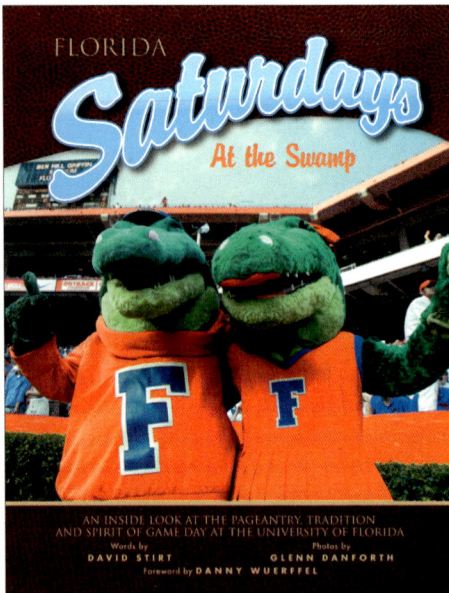